IMMERSION
Bible Studies

MARK

Praise for IMMERSION

"IMMERSION BIBLE STUDIES is a powerful tool in helping readers to hear God speak through Scripture and to experience a deeper faith as a result."
Adam Hamilton, author of *24 Hours That Changed the World*

"This unique Bible study makes Scripture come alive for students. Through the study, students are invited to move beyond the head into the heart of faith."
Bishop Joseph W. Walker, author of *Love and Intimacy*

"This beautiful series helps readers become fluent in the words and thoughts of God, for purposes of illumination, strength building, and developing a closer walk with the One who loves us so."
Laurie Beth Jones, author of *Jesus, CEO* and *The Path*

"I highly commend to you IMMERSION BIBLE STUDIES, which tells us what the Bible teaches and how to apply it personally."
John Ed Mathison, author of *Treasures of the Transformed Life*

"The IMMERSION BIBLE STUDIES series is no less than a game changer. It ignites the purpose and power of Scripture by showing us how to do more than just know God or love God; it gives us the tools to love like God as well."
Shane Stanford, author of *You Can't Do Everything . . . So Do Something*

IMMERSION
Bible Studies

MARK

Emerson B. Powery

Abingdon Press

Nashville

MARK
IMMERSION BIBLE STUDIES
by Emerson B. Powery

Library of Congress Cataloging-in-Publication Data
Powery, Emerson B.
  Mark / Emerson B. Powery.
    p. cm. —(Immersion Bible studies)
    ISBN 978-1-4267-0916-6 (curriculum—printed/text plus-cover, adhesive - perfect binding : alk. paper)
    1. Bible. N.T. Mark—Textbooks. I. Title.
  BS2586.P68 2010
  226.3'06—dc22
                          2010039857

Editor: Jack A. Keller, Jr.
Leader Guide Writer: Martha Bettis Gee

11 12 13 14 15 16 17 18 19 20—10 9 8 7 6 5 4 3 2 1

Manufactured in the United States of America

Contents

REVIEW TEAM

IMMERSION BIBLE STUDIES

*A fresh new look at the Bible, from beginning to end,
and what it means in your life.*

Welcome to IMMERSION!

We've asked some of the leading Bible scholars, teachers, and pastors to help us with a new kind of Bible study. IMMERSION remains true to Scripture but always asks, "Where are you in your life? What do you struggle with? What makes you rejoice?" Then it helps you read the Scriptures to discover their deep, abiding truths. IMMERSION is about God and God's Word, and it is also about you—not just your thoughts, but your feelings and your faith.

In each study you will prayerfully read the Scripture and reflect on it. Then you will engage it in three ways:

Claim Your Story
> Through stories and questions, think about your life, with its struggles and joys.

Enter the Bible Story
> Explore Scripture and consider what God is saying to you.

Live the Story
> Reflect on what you have discovered, and put it into practice in your life.

MARK

IMMERSION makes use of an exciting new translation of Scripture, the Common English Bible (CEB). The CEB and IMMERSION BIBLE STUDIES will offer adults:

- the emotional expectation to find the love of God
- the rational expectation to find the knowledge of God
- reliable, genuine, and credible power to transform lives
- clarity of language

Whether you are using the Common English Bible or another translation, IMMERSION BIBLE STUDIES will offer a refreshing plunge into God's Word, your life, and your life with God.

1.

Jesus' Authority as Son of God

Mark 1:1-20; 3:13-19

Claim Your Story

Make a mental list of persons in our society—or better, in your particular community—who exercise some measure of authority. What roles do those persons play? Are they coaches? Teachers? Police officers? Elected officials? Parents or guardians? Lawyers? Judges? Big Brothers? Big Sisters? Guidance counselors? Researchers? Food inspectors? Clergy? Contractors? Doctors? Business executives or managers? Union leaders? Investment bankers? Regulatory officials?

Does the word *authority* have positive or negative connotations for you? What positive examples of authority have you heard about or observed? What abuses of authority have you heard about or observed? What do you think accounts for the difference? Have you heard of situations in which people have performed surprising acts in the name of religious authority? Whether you agree or not with the action that was carried out, what were your reactions to the claim that the act was performed in the name of God?

The issue of authority was critical in the opening chapters of Jesus' mission. From where did his authority come? Why did the mainstream religious authorities not easily validate his authority?

What does Scripture have to say about Jesus' authority? What does Scripture say about the authority granted to his followers?

Enter the Bible Story

The opening of the Gospel of Mark is about authority. Of course, it was a particular authority that Mark had in mind. He was writing a story about the authority of Jesus, who was (and is), as the opening verse suggests, God's Son. Now that is authority! The title "God's Son" is quite rare in the Gospel of Mark. Jesus never refers to himself in this way. In Mark he prefers to use another title for himself, the "Human One" (CEB) or "Son of Man" (NRSV). No *human* figure recognizes Jesus as the Son of God until the Roman centurion confesses Jesus as God's Son at Jesus' death (15:39). For Mark, Jesus' ultimate authority as God's Son was closely associated with his ultimate sacrifice.

The discussion on authority does not end with the opening words of this Gospel. Mark linked the telling of his story with Isaiah's story. He wanted to assure his readers that the story he was about to relay was one

---

Across the Testaments

Mark's Use of Isaiah

Mark began his story with a citation from Scripture, making a connection to the Book of Isaiah to describe John's activity. This scriptural text establishes the authority of John's appearance. Although "the prophecy of Isaiah" is listed as the source of this citation, verses 2-3 are a conflation of two or three texts: Exodus 23:20, Malachi 3:1, and Isaiah 40:3. Other Jews, such as the Essenes in Qumran (a community on the northwest shore of the Dead Sea), also read Isaiah 40 as a sign of their present condition. For this Jewish sect, this passage highlighted their communal activity depicting the way in the desert. Their preparation, in the wilderness, included a constant reading and study of the Law. In Mark's interpretation of Isaiah 40, John's preaching (and Jesus' preaching) was preparation for the way. For Mark, this way took on a technical meaning as well, as the way to the cross (see 1:2-3; 8:27; 9:33-34; 10:32). It was also a way that caused Jesus, and John, to stay involved in the everyday affairs of the mainstream. That is, unlike the residents of Qumran, they did not understand Isaiah 40 as a message to relocate to the desert in order to maintain their faith. Their mission kept them among the local villages and near the city of Jerusalem.

that had ancient roots. In the first-century world, new stories needed to have connections to the past to be trustworthy. Old was better! So Mark informed his readers that the coming of Jesus was tied directly to a plan that God had had in place for a long time. Again, for Mark, this helped to establish Jesus' authority.

The other major point of authority was Jesus' association with John, who arrived on the scene as one who was already so completely established as an authoritative figure that "all the people of Jerusalem" were going out to the wilderness—not necessarily a safe place—to hear John's message (Mark 1:4-8). We know from sources outside the New Testament, such as the ancient Jewish historian Josephus, that John was a very popular Jewish figure.

We even learn from Mark (later in the story) that John, too, had disciples who would eventually come to bury him when he died (see Mark 6:29). Not only did Isaiah's story point to the significance of John's activity for the coming reign of God, helping to establish John's authority, Jesus would join the large group of people who accepted John's authority by receiving his baptism. Jesus' willingness to receive John's baptism would cause some angst among other early Christians reflecting on this tradition, however.

Mark's description of Jesus' baptism by John is the most straightforward account of any of the Gospel versions. Jesus came to John, and the baptizer performed this exclusive act. More important than the baptism was what happened at the moment of the baptism, an experience that, according to Mark, only Jesus witnessed: God's Spirit descended from heaven and landed on him. The Greek actually uses the preposition *eis* ("into") for the direction of the Spirit's movement. That is, the Holy Spirit *entered* Jesus; and he then became the Spirit-empowered agent of God, who would fight against the evil forces in the world (as the Gospel of Mark continues). Finally, God (Mark preferred the euphemism "a voice from heaven" [1:11].) spoke directly to Jesus and claimed him as a beloved son. Even the baptism was an event showing readers Jesus' authority.

This Gospel is not a suspense story that keeps the identity of the lead character in check until some significant life-altering moment occurs in the protagonist's life. This is not a story that will gradually reveal Jesus' identity as we continue to read. Rather, the Gospel of Mark provides this crucial apocalyptic moment (that is, the heavens splitting) at the beginning of the story. Jesus' identity is clear from the opening verses. What will be suspenseful is how others—Jesus' family, disciples, religious authorities, Rome—react to him, his message, and his mission. Indeed, at the baptism, Jesus is declared to be God's Son.

About the Scripture

Jesus' Baptism According to the Synoptic Gospels

Mark's Gospel is the earliest written Gospel and the least reluctant to describe John's baptism of Jesus (Mark 1:9). Matthew's Gospel depicts an explicit event of baptism, but only after John expresses unwillingness: "I need to be baptized by you, yet you come to me?" Jesus responds that the baptism is a necessary act of righteousness (Matthew 3:13-15). The Gospels of Luke and John only provide implicit information regarding Jesus' baptism by John. In Luke, it seems as if John has been imprisoned before Jesus receives baptism (see Luke 3:19-21). And, in John, there is a lengthy description of John's awareness of the coming "Lamb of God" but no direct contact between him and Jesus for a baptism to occur. John the Baptist is primarily a witness in John's Gospel and not the baptizer of Jesus. If Mark is first and John is last, the Gospel writers grew increasingly reticent about describing Jesus' baptism by John, since the one who is "greater" is expected to perform baptisms. This event was apparently a point of tension for later Christians.

Immediately following God granting Jesus his authoritative role as Son, Jesus experienced his first challenge: a wilderness test (Mark 1:12-13). In biblical history, such a test in the desert regions recalled the sojourn and test of the people of Israel in the story of the Exodus. Mark's original audience would certainly have caught the thematic link. Jesus was one who had been tested as God's other son, Israel, was tested; and Jesus passed the test. In Mark's account (unlike Matthew's and Luke's), the details of Jesus' temptation are omitted. The specific temptation is not the focus of this confrontation with Satan. Rather, it is enough to know that it happened and Jesus succeeded. What we do not want to miss is that the Spirit of God initiated the entire test: "At once the Spirit forced Jesus out into the wilderness" (1:12). In the Gospel of Mark, the tests that came into Jesus' life were often initiated by God. In this instance, as in many to come, Jesus would overcome.

We, too, may experience tests in our spiritual journeys. Frequently, those tests come in order to prepare us for future challenges. Sometimes those tests are part of God's plans for us. God may even initiate them. Accepting that possibility is often difficult because of our theological perspective. We tend to assume that because we are God's children, no obstacles will ever come our way. From experience, however, we know this is not to be the case. In this opening story of Jesus' wilderness test, Jesus' life is a perfect example of how some challenges come to us from God. In such times a discerning spirit will be crucial to enable us to grasp what we need to learn from these situations in life. Thankfully, we know that God will not test us beyond what we are capable of handling.

Jesus' opening words in Mark's story were an announcement of God's good news (1:14-15). As the one who had been anointed by God, Jesus had the authority to proclaim such a message. And it was indeed good news. Even so, as the temptation scene suggests, it was not a message that would go unchallenged. Nor would the resistance cease any time soon. John's arrest, just before Jesus began his public mission (see 1:14), showed that a potentially ominous future awaited anyone who continued on the path of attempting to carry out God's justice-oriented activity in the world. Later in the narrative (6:14-29), Mark will explore John's arrest and death for the implications of Jesus' own activity and that of his followers. John's death, as his arrest, hints at a threatening future for anyone who follows God.

Following his opening public announcement of God's good news, Jesus' first public activity was to call a few good people (Mark 1:16-20). Jesus had a mission in mind, and he did not intend to carry out this task alone. He was apparently mindful of the enormity of the calling on his life and his mission in the world. Unlike many other well-known rabbis of the day, Jesus sought out followers. He did not wait for them to become attracted to his mission. Apparently, Jesus already had begun the strategic work of recognizing the need for other agents in the field. He did not hesitate, according to Mark's Gospel, to locate some capable fishermen to start to develop his group.

The fact that these fishermen left their day jobs was astounding in the context of first-century life. James and John left behind financial security. They were "repairing the fishing nets" (Mark 1:19) that were worn out from successful catches. Their father also had "hired workers" (1:20) with him. This was a small but successful business enterprise that Zebedee was running along the coasts of the Galilean sea. Yet James and John left it behind to follow the authoritative presence of Jesus.

More culturally surprising than leaving behind the business is that James and John were abandoning their father. Abandoning one's family in this way was a striking example of what Jesus would teach later in this Gospel: "I assure you that anyone who has left house, brothers, sisters, mother, father, children, or farms because of me and because of the good news will receive a hundred times as much now in this life" (Mark 10:29-30). Even today, there are often costs associated with following Jesus. Granted, Christianity is respected widely in the West and particularly in the USA. But many Christian families still discourage or, at least, frown on family members if they decide to go into full-time ministry. To leave a good job in midlife in order to attend seminary seems unwise. To be honest, I myself discourage my own children from thinking about choosing the ministry as their profession. While it may not be culturally disadvantageous, it is certainly a professional choice that can come with a lot of headaches. The itinerant nature of the ministerial calling can be daunting for families and hard on their relationships.

Despite the thematic focus of Mark's opening as I discuss it here, the word *authority* (*exousia* in Greek) does not occur until Mark 1:22. At that point, it is explicit: "He was teaching them with authority, not like the legal experts." Yet the opening is also really about Jesus' authority in and of itself. In the opening preface, Mark shows us the authority Jesus had rather than explicitly stating it; and it is an authority he had in relationship to the scriptural story, John's story, and God's story.

With authority comes responsibility. This was no less the case for Jesus' initial followers than it is for us. Jesus assigned them specific duties (Mark 3:13-19): to be present with him, to continue to pass along his message (to preach God's reign in the world), and to continue to carry out his activities (to exorcise demons). The authority Jesus gave was to say what he said, do what he did, and (simply) to be in community with him. Oftentimes, this last part is overlooked. Part of the reason for that oversight is because the statement "he appointed them to be with him" (3:14) is unique to Mark's Gospel. Neither Matthew nor Luke records it in their version of Jesus' appointment of the Twelve. In Mark, Jesus did not just call people in order to carry out a specific mission. He also called them "to be with him." Jesus understood the value of friendship and solidarity. Being with him and being with each other is part of what it means to be disciples of Jesus Christ.

Live the Story

What authority does Jesus have in our lives? If we consider ourselves to be followers of Jesus, what does that really mean to us in the twenty-first century? How does that affect our decisions to share in the events of our cities or engage our local communities? How does it shape the relationships we have with our families and friends?

From Mark we learn that ultimately Jesus' authority was derived from God, and it was something that he shared with his followers so that they would continue to carry out his mission of peace in the world during his absence (Mark 1:16-20; 3:13-19). So what does this have to do with us?

I would like to think that as a community of Christ followers, we each have responsibilities. But the ways we live out these responsibilities need not be the same. Furthermore, these responsibilities tend to require us to reach outside of church communities. Jesus was actually engaged in a mission that took him outside of the synagogues most of the time. He did not ignore the centers of religious instruction (see Mark 1:21-27), but his influence was not confined there either.

Let's take the specific assignments Jesus gave the disciples (Mark 3:14-15) and think about them as three different types of people in our faith communities. Some of us will be people whose primary role is simply "to be with him." These people are not pious simply for piety's sake. Rather, they carry all members of our community in their prayers and religious walks. They are constantly mindful of the spiritual challenges we face in the world. Second, some of us will be people who "preach" Jesus' message. This may be of the formal kind like the leaders in our congregations who guide us through sermons, Bible studies, and other devotional literature. But this may also include those persons responsible for presenting Christian faith in broader conversations, for example, in interreligious dialogues. This, too, is a type of preaching. Finally, our third group of people will be those who are given authority "to throw out demons." These people are the ones among us who are more action oriented. They use their hands as the gift God has given them; and they serve God through working in soup kitchens, building homes for the impoverished, and offering the cup of cold water to the thirsty traveler. Indeed, today demons exist in various forms, including the structures that separate those who have from those who have much less.

No one of these roles is sufficient by itself, which is why I like to think in terms of the community of followers of Jesus. Each of us needs the other to fulfill the mission in the world that Jesus gave us all. Equally important, Jesus gave us the authority, through the power of God's Spirit, to continue to serve God in these various ways. Consider thoughtfully and prayerfully what God may be calling you to do to fulfill the mission Jesus has given us.

Jesus' Authority and Power Revealed in Healings

Mark 2:1-12; 3:1-6; 5:1-20; 5:21-43; 6:53-56;
7:24-30; 7:31-37; 8:22-26; 9:14-29; 10:46-52

Claim Your Story

Have you or anyone close to you ever experienced a healing in your life? If so, was it a sudden process or a lengthy one? Were others involved, or was it a supernatural healing? Were doctors and other health care professionals involved in the process? Were friends and family involved? If so, to what extent? In any case, did you feel God's presence in the process?

Do you know of people who have *not* found the healing they desire? Have you (or anyone you know) lived with pain, physical or emotional, all your life and wondered why God has not provided healing? If so, has it been an isolating experience? Does the idea of healing carry a negative or a positive connotation for you or for others close to you? Do you wonder if God has chosen not to heal some people? If so, is it a function of the way they conduct their lives? Is it a result of their lack of faith?

Healing is the restoration of something that has been damaged. Consider the different types of healing that can occur in your life: physical, mental, emotional, and the healing of your faith. What kinds of healings do you sense the most in your community? in your household? for you personally?

Enter the Bible Story

Around 200 B.C., an ancient Jewish philosopher and teacher offered a defense of the trained physician: "Honor physicians for their services, for the LORD created them" (Ben Sira 38:1, NRSV). John Wesley frequently cited Ben Sira's words in his discussions of healing and health. These words would have been common knowledge among first-century A.D. Jews. Yet Jesus was no common medical practitioner, nor was he a trained physician. How would Jesus' healings have been understood in the first century? Perhaps more importantly, what do Jesus' healings have to do with the contemporary church?

The Christian tradition has provided at least two extreme responses on healings: everything and nothing at all. Let's begin with the latter. According to this view, Jesus' healings were a first-century phenomenon that was unique to Jesus and his immediate followers (as reported in the Book of Acts) in early Christianity. Beyond that initial period of the spreading of the gospel (when such miracles were necessary for evangelization), they were and are no longer essential to advance the cause of Christ. On the other hand, another wing within Christianity (especially since the early twentieth century) emphasizes healings as essential representations of the continuing vibrancy of the Christian movement. This segment argues, additionally, that the failure of contemporary Christians to experience this evidence of God's power is a clear sign of our lack of faith. Those who "live right" or have sufficient faith, it is often claimed, will secure their healing. Both positions are extreme, and extremely mistaken, about the function of Jesus' healings for the Christian movement.

In the biblical narratives, healings were usually about something more than the healings themselves. Do not get me wrong; the healed individual certainly recognized the personal benefit she or he received. I am confident that Jesus cared for the suffering individual who obtained this care and restoration. But the authors who told these stories generally did so for other reasons than simply to report that Jesus healed this or that person. That is, it was not just a statement about Jesus' power or authority, though it was certainly about that too. Never in Mark (or in any of the other three

Gospels) do we read of anyone confessing Jesus as God's Son or Messiah after a healing. The only exception to this point would be the unclean spirit who possessed humans (Mark 1:23-24). But this was the unclean spirit speaking and not the human agent. Instead, the stories revealed Jesus to be a healer, and a popular one at that. The ancillary issue, on the other hand, was one that has implications for Jesus' wider mission at the point of the healing.

Healing and Social Isolation

What are some of these wider issues that are central to the healing stories of Jesus? Take, for example, the healing of a man with a skin disease (Mark 1:40-45). This was a story about this one man's healing; but it was also a story about the nature of such diseases, traditionally classified as leprosy. In Leviticus 13–14, the law stipulated that people with skin diseases should be quarantined for weeklong periods because they were considered religiously unclean. The priest, according to the Torah, functioned as the medical examiner who determined the effect of the disease. After a seven-day period, the person would be examined again. If the priest determined that the individual had a leprous disease, this person would be ostracized from the community and was required to announce "Unclean! unclean!" whenever she or he approached others in the village (Leviticus 13:45). According to the law, "They are unclean. They must live alone outside the camp" (13:46). Social isolation was the outcome of this disease, and Jesus became angry about it.

Jesus recognized the importance of this person's cleanliness to the whole community. That is, Jesus did not say, "You are clean despite your disease," even though Jesus' touch may have implied this idea. Rather, Jesus healed him of his disease before sending the man to the priests for a check-up. And it was the priests who would have a say in the outcome of this man's cleansing. Here Jesus was a law-abiding healer/prophet who on the one hand was faithful to the traditions of the ancestors (Show the priest and bring what is required.) yet on the other hand did not follow the rules in every detail (He touched the man with a skin disease and ignored the traditional methods for cleansing.).

Healing and the Forgiveness of Sins

Or, take the very next story in Mark (2:1-12): the healing of a paralyzed man. Unlike the unnamed person with a skin disease, this paralyzed man had friends, a lot of friends. As Mark put it, the man had enough friends to carry him and his mat to the top of a roof, remove a portion of the roof, and lower the man down into the crowd where Jesus was. This was not a story about social isolation. This man was not suffering alone in this tiny first-century village. Furthermore, Jesus recognized the faith of these people (2:5), clearly evident in their extraordinary actions: tearing the roof off of someone's house. But this story was also not about this individual's healing, though he eventually received one. It was a story about Jesus' authority to forgive sins (2:5). This priestly act was an offense to the religious establishment. They said that Jesus was "insulting God" (2:7). Only God or God's priests should have had this kind of authority. In the end, Jesus not only forgave the man's sins but also healed his body.

Healing and Overcoming Ethnic and Cultural Boundaries

Consider one of my favorite healing stories: the Syrophoenician woman's request for her daughter's healing (Mark 7:24-30). Eventually, from a distance, the daughter's demon would be sent away from her. The account, however, was unquestionably not written just to prove that Jesus could heal from a distance. Mark's literary placement of this story provides insight into how we should interpret it. In the previous narrative (7:1-23), Jesus had a debate with some Pharisees about the practice of eating with unwashed hands; and then the argument shifted to a discussion of the nature of food itself—whether specific foods should be considered religiously unclean. This debate had implications for Jesus' mission: Would boundaries continue to separate Jews from non-Jews? If so, what would be the symbols of those boundaries? Would food be such a symbol? Jesus' response to the specific questions was to challenge both issues. Even the requirement of carefully, ritually washing hands before eating, which was an ancient tradition of the elders, should not be placed above other concerns. And according to Mark, Jesus declared that "no food could contaminate a person in God's sight" (7:19). Following Jesus' debate with the

Pharisees and scribes, Mark reported the story about Jesus' encounter with this Greek woman. So it was not just about *food*; it was also about *people*. This story about an exorcism from a distance was a story about something more than the healing itself. It was about tearing down ethnic and cultural boundaries, and Jesus was leading the way.

But what about the healings themselves? Don't they teach us anything about Jesus and the practice of healing? They certainly do. Jesus healed people in a variety of ways. In addition, the Gospels also provide information on what people thought about the origins of illness. Some of the traditional ideas, like a theology of retribution, still existed among some first-century Jews. The idea that God blessed only those who trusted in God and harmed those who did not had a long history in Jewish theology, a way of thinking that was challenged by the Book of Job. But that challenge to this traditional perspective did not do away with this idea among many Jews. For example, notice the perspective of Ben Sira (c. 200 B.C.). On the one hand, the author praised the physician as one who worked in conjunction with God to heal and to take away pain (38:1-7). On the other hand, according to this same author, illnesses derived from sin (38:10-11).

This same idea still lingered in the first-century world. Notice two stories in John's Gospel. In one account (John 5), shortly after healing a paralyzed man, Jesus encountered him again and warned him, "Don't sin anymore in case something worse happens to you" (5:14). Yet, a few chapters later (John 9), Jesus called into question a similar perspective when his disciples asked, "Who sinned so that he was born blind, this man or his parents?" (9:2). Significantly, Jesus challenged the conception that sin was the cause of this man's blindness: "Neither he nor his parents [sinned]. This happened so that God's mighty works might be displayed in him" (9:3). These stories in John's Gospel let us know that the traditional theology of retribution was still in the ethos of the first century. But it was not the only idea that people held in regard to illnesses and diseases.

When we turn back to Mark's Gospel, tracing the origins of diseases is less clear. There are no explicit stories in which sin is the primary explanation given as the root of the sickness. Suffering is not the fault of the

Ben Sira 38:1-15

Honor physicians for their services, for the LORD created them;
    for their gift of healing comes from the Most High,
    and they are rewarded by the king.
The skill of physicians makes them distinguished,
    and in the presence of the great they are admired.
The LORD created medicines out of the earth,
    and the sensible will not despise them.
Was not water made sweet with a tree in order that
    its power might be known?
And he gave skill to human beings that he might be
    glorified in his marvelous works.
By them the physician heals and takes away pain;
    the pharmacist makes a mixture from them.
God's works will never be finished;
    and from him health spreads over all the earth.
My child, when you are ill, do not delay,
    but pray to the LORD, and he will heal you.
Give up your faults and direct your hands rightly,
    and cleanse your heart from all sin.
Offer a sweet-smelling sacrifice, and a memorial portion of
    choice flour,
    and pour oil on your offering, as much as you can afford.
Then give the physician his place, for the LORD created him;
    do not let him leave you, for you need him.
There may come a time when recovery lies in the hands of
    physicians,
    for they too pray to the LORD that he grant them success in
    diagnosis and in healing, for the sake of preserving life.
He who sins against his Maker, will be defiant toward
    the physician. (NRSV)

victims. Unlike John, Mark omitted any such discussion, strongly imply-ing that there were a variety of perspectives on the origin of illnesses.

What about the issue of faith and healing? Was faith always neces-sary? When we read many of the stories in Mark's Gospel, we may get the impression that the faith of the one healed was always necessary to the process. Faith was often described as part of the process (see Mark 5:34; 10:52), but it was not always the faith of the individual that was mentioned. Sometimes it was the faith of others, like the friends of the man who was paralyzed (2:5), which led to Jesus' healing activity. Finally, to consider the full record in Mark's Gospel, there were also a number of healings in which no faith was mentioned at all (for example, 1:30-31; 3:5). On this last point, this was a major element of the story when Jesus came into his hometown synagogue (6:1-6). Jesus was shocked at the lack of faith he witnessed among his family and friends, those who had known him for a longer period of time. Yet he still decided to heal a few people (6:5-6). Jesus had the sovereign power to do just that despite the presence of unbelief. So Mark did not portray some consistent pattern that contemporary Christians simply need to follow. Rather, the agent of God could heal in a variety of ways with or without the presence of belief. God is sovereign!

Live the Story

What should we take away from these stories of healing? What do Jesus' first-century healings have to do with us, a broken and yet empowered people? What is the Spirit saying to the church and society?

How does the community of faith respond to the needs of others? First, like the friends of the unnamed man who was formerly paralyzed, we need to be people willing to have enough faith—for the sake of others—for our faith to shape our actions because when Jesus saw their faith, he acted. This type of communal faith may take all kinds of directions in the contemporary world. The recent crisis in Haiti is one example. The extraordinary story of the Harvard-trained physician Dr. Paul Farmer, as told in Tracey Kidder's best-selling book *Mountains Beyond Mountains*, is one such account of the various ways people act on their faith. Like Farmer, who established medical clinics in Haiti (and elsewhere) before the recent crisis, the Christian community needs to be part of the healing process. We should be part of proactive attempts to participate in God's active healing of the world's brokenness, including the disparities that lead to so many of the small, treatable diseases that still plague large segments of our world's communities.

What about those individuals among us who continue to suffer physically or emotionally from some unending ailment? We learn from these stories that suffering need not isolate anyone any longer. Nor is it a question of one's faith (or lack thereof). God does not treat people vindictively because of some action of theirs in the past. God loves us and cares for us. On some issues, the mysteries of God go beyond our understanding.

3.
Jesus' Authority and Power Revealed in Nature Miracles

Mark 4:35-41; 6:30-44; 6:45-52; 8:1-10; 9:2-8

Claim Your Story

What is a miracle? Are miracles strictly acts of God? *Merriam-Webster's Collegiate Dictionary*, Tenth Edition, defines a miracle as "1. an extraordinary event manifesting divine intervention in human affairs" or "2. An extremely outstanding or unusual event, thing, or accomplishment."

Have you ever witnessed a miracle? Have you been an integral part of one? If so, was it God's plan to include you in the miracle? How does God intend for us to participate in miracles? Why does God include us in the miracles of others?

How often do you experience miracles? How often do you witness miracles occurring for others around you? What connotations does the idea of miracles have? Are they all positive? Do any negative ones come to mind? Is the term "miracle" used too frequently in your community? Is it not used enough? Is the term one of comfort? Is it one of hope or one of improbability? Are individuals in your community skeptical of miracles?

The Gospel of Mark portrays Jesus as a miracle worker. In Chapter 2, we examined some of Jesus' miracles of *healing*. In this chapter, let's consider what Mark has to say about what might be called the *nature* miracles of Jesus.

Enter the Bible Story

Unlike the healings described in the Gospels, Jesus' miraculous power over nature rarely attracted attention. Why was this the case? What purpose must this power have served? Why did Jesus reserve demonstrations of his power over nature only for his closest followers? Let's take a quick survey through the stories of the Gospel of Mark in which the author describes Jesus' extraordinary power over natural forces.

Let's face it; the disciples, even though they had been following Jesus for a while, did not fully understand whom they were following. By the time we get to Jesus' first nature miracle in the Gospel of Mark (4:35-41), the disciples have committed themselves to Jesus even if they were unsure about his entire mission. Mark describes the scene in which Jesus calmed violent winds. Jesus was resting; the disciples were battling the natural forces of chaotic waves on the Sea of Galilee. The disciples could not understand why Jesus was not helping them. At least he could have helped bail out the water that was quickly filling their boat. It is the way they questioned Jesus, however, that is disturbing: "Teacher, don't you care . . . ?" (4:38).

"Don't you care?" Of course, we know the whole story; so it is hard to grasp the sense of panic that gripped the disciples. They had witnessed the expression of Jesus' concern for friends, family, and strangers with his healing touches and comforting words. Now *they* needed his help desperately, and he was sleeping.

Finally, he woke up. But what they got was not what they were expecting. Jesus told the wind and waves to calm down. And they did! Immediately! Not only did Jesus express his care for the disciples by miraculously altering their situation, he also had his own question for them: "Don't you have faith yet?" (Mark 4:40). Wow! That had to strike them right in the heart. They were shocked, and they expressed it clearly: "Who then is this [person]?" (4:41). They immediately recognized, for the first time, that Jesus was someone more than the healer-teacher with whom they had been hanging out. They had a right to be afraid.

Just a few chapters later, the disciples would have another revelatory moment on the same lake (Mark 6:45-52). Jesus' walk on the water followed directly after another miracle in Mark, the first miraculous feeding of a large crowd (6:30-44), which we will discuss below. No one except the disciples had any clue about Jesus' miraculous power. Jesus revealed his

Across the Testaments

Jonah and Jesus

Mark's account of Jesus sleeping in the stern of the boat while his disciples panicked during a ferocious storm may have reminded Mark's audience of a parallel story about Jonah. Jonah was fast asleep during a terrible storm until the ship's captain awakened him, insisting that Jonah pray to God for deliverance (Jonah 1:4-6). At that point the parallel breaks down, since Jesus did not pray for God's protection but issued direct commands to the wind and water. Clearly, Mark was (and is) telling his readers that Jesus was more than a prophet.

power over nature—a sign that revealed his divine authority—*only to the disciples* (and readers of Mark's Gospel). Such miracles were not designed as evangelistic tools, to be proof to outsiders. God's agent did not work that way. In the Gospel of Mark, it was only the Pharisees—religious opponents of Jesus—who sought signs (see 8:11). Those who wish to turn the miraculous power of God into a circus sideshow have misunderstood the function of this power in the Christian community. These signs, in the scriptural witness, are provided to *increase* faith, not to *initiate* faith.

In Mark's second story about Jesus' control over the sea (6:45-52), Jesus was not in the boat with the disciples but rather strolled on the water as if it were solid ground. In fact, as the story goes in Mark, "Jesus made his disciples get into a boat and go ahead to the other side of the lake" (6:45), thus sending them into the storm. (This should remind us of the Spirit driving Jesus into the "storm" of the wilderness temptation.) In contemporary art, the scene depicted is usually derived from Matthew's version, which included Peter's bold attempt to walk on the water. Peter's courageous act is absent from Mark's version, so we should focus our interpretation elsewhere.

The Gospel of Mark emphasizes that "seeing him was terrifying to all of them" (6:50), the phrase "all of them" being omitted in Matthew. *All* the disciples were amazed at what they were experiencing. Unlike the earlier sea miracle, which ended with an appropriate question about Jesus' identity, this sea story ended with Mark's assessment that "their hearts had

Across the Testaments

God's Power Over the Sea

In many Old Testament passages, the sea represents chaos and danger. One dimension of God's power is the divine ability to bring order and rescue out of chaos. Jesus' power of command over a storm and his ability to walk on the water would likely have reminded Mark's readers of Psalm 107:23-32:

Some of the redeemed had gone out on the ocean in ships,
making their living on the high seas.
They saw what the LORD had made;
they saw his wondrous works in the depths of the sea.
God spoke and stirred up a storm
that brought the waves up high.
The waves went as high as the sky, they crashed down to the depths.
The sailors' courage melted at this terrible situation.
They staggered and stumbled around like they were drunk.
None of their skill was of any help.
So they cried out to the LORD in their distress,
and God brought them out safe from their desperate circumstances.
God quieted the storm to a whisper;
the sea's waves were hushed.
So they rejoiced because the waves had calmed down;
then God led them to the harbor they were hoping for.
Let them thank the LORD for his faithful love
and his wondrous works for all people.
Let them exalt God in the congregation of the people,
and praise God in the assembly of the elders.

been changed so that they resisted God's ways" (6:52). Jesus' desire to reveal himself (slowly) to the disciples by means of his powerful acts over nature fell on deaf ears, dull eyes, and "hardened" hearts (NRSV). Jesus' revelation of his power over nature did not lead to (more) faith from his disciples; it led to more fear, the kind that was associated with the unbelieving Pharisees. This is, in some respects, a caution about Christian faith that is completely dependent on miracles. The miraculous, or the expectancy of the miraculous as the primary way that God acts, often leads to more conflict and fear than long-term faith. Possibly, this is another reason Jesus reserved demonstrations of such miraculous power only for his close followers.

The Gospel of Mark does mention one odd feature. In 6:48, as Jesus saw what was happening to the disciples, "he came to them, walking on the lake"; and, as only Mark puts it, "He intended to pass by them" (6:48). Oddly, it appears that Jesus had no intention of coming directly to them. He would pass "alongside them" (the literal meaning of the Greek),[1] perhaps to watch over them and protect them, without their notice. As one prominent Markan scholar, Joel Marcus, rightly recognizes, Jesus "wishes to pass the disciples by for their own good, to give them a full revelation of his identity, but he cannot do so because of their terror and incomprehension."[2] Indeed, we see what happened when they actually saw him: *They were more frightened of him than of the storm.* "They thought he was a ghost" (6:49). This Jesus was so much not like them at all. Neither is he like us! Because we cannot contain Jesus in our preconceived notions and expectations, Jesus remains free to walk to our boats when he chooses, to still the storm in his own time, and to calm our fears.

Jesus' compassion reaches not just particular individuals, but everyone. The grand feedings of large crowds in Mark's Gospel are excellent examples of this quality of Jesus. When the first significant crowd came out to Jesus from various surrounding villages, Jesus "had compassion on them because they were like sheep without a shepherd" (Mark 6:34). A few chapters later, another large crowd gathered (on the other side of the lake); and Jesus responded, "I feel sorry for the crowd because they have . . . nothing to eat" (8:2). In both cases, Jesus used what his disciples possessed to perform these grand miracles. Jesus utilized what was available to him in the hands of those who had prepared for the journey.

No one in the crowd, as far as we are told, noticed what Jesus was up to, however. No one in the crowd offered any confession that was generated by Jesus' extraordinary act. Look at the stories for yourself and you will not find any crowd reaction to their satisfied bellies and souls. The crowd did not gather because Jesus proved who he was by demonstrating his power over natural forces. The crowd gathered to hear stories about the way God works in the world and to have their illnesses cured. These miracles became a critical lesson for the disciples (see, for instance, Mark 8:14-21), who were generally surprised one moment and oblivious the next.

The scene most likely to draw attention to the unusual identity of Jesus is reported in Mark 9:2-8. The Transfiguration (*metemorphothe*, from which we get our English word *metamorphosis*), occurred in two ways: (1) his apparel became "amazingly bright" (Mark 9:3); and (2) two ancient biblical heroes, Elijah and Moses, appeared (9:4). Yet Peter still recognized Jesus (calling him "Rabbi" [9:5]) and attempted to inquire about the symbolic importance of the occasion.

Across the Testaments

Moses and Elijah

The appearance of Elijah and Moses would have been a clue for ancient observers and readers that some special end-time event was occurring. In light of each figure's mysterious death/disappearance, it was thought that Moses and Elijah would reappear in the messianic age. In Deuteronomy, Moses himself announced such an appearance of a Moses-like figure: "The LORD your God will raise up a prophet like me from your community, from your fellow Israelites. He's the one you must listen to" (18:15). The prophet Malachi recalled Moses' words: "Remember the Instruction of Moses, my servant, to whom I gave Instruction and rules for all Israel at Horeb. Look, I am sending Elijah the prophet to you, before the great and terrifying day of the LORD arrives" (Malachi 4:4-5). The author of the final book of the New Testament may also be alluding to their end-time appearance in the reference to the "two witnesses" of Revelation 11. Certainly, these traditions were part of what triggered Peter's desire to build "three shrines" (Mark 9:5), perhaps an attempt to mark symbolically the revelatory event.

In lieu of Jesus' response, "a voice spoke from the cloud" and responded to Peter and the others with another statement of identity: "This is my Son, whom I dearly love" (Mark 9:7). The reader is reminded of Jesus' baptism (in Mark 1), where "a voice from heaven" also spoke with the same supporting claim. The authoritative relationship between God and Jesus was reinforced in this revelatory, metamorphic experience. No event in Mark's Gospel equals the transfiguration scene in terms of the revelation of Jesus' identity. The reader cannot help but recognize in this event a foreshadowing of the post-resurrection Jesus. As Jesus claimed in the preceding (and first) prediction and would repeat in the next two, he was the kind of messianic figure who would "after three days, rise from the dead" (Mark 8:31). The Transfiguration, at least for the three witnesses and readers, lent substantive hope to this possibility of a resurrected Lord.

The nature miracles of Jesus were reserved for Jesus' closest followers. Rarely, if ever, do we find Jesus revealing publicly this type of divine power in large crowds. The stories about Jesus' power over nature were reserved, according to Mark, for those who had already begun the journey with Jesus. They were for those who had already expressed some faith, that is, they were for those who had made initial commitments to support Jesus' mission. Yet these miracles still continued to confront the faith of these close followers in order to challenge them to deepen their trust in God and God's work in the world.

Live the Story

Jesus' nature miracles in the Gospel of Mark, as I have noted above, were not tools for evangelism so much as they were a way of reaching those who had already begun the journey with Jesus, inviting (and challenging!) them to trust God more deeply. Where are the places in your life that resonate with the needs of Jesus' closest followers and with Jesus' response to those needs? What are the storms that frighten you? What might it mean for Jesus to calm those storms? How does Jesus encourage and comfort you? Jesus responded to the hunger of the crowds with compassion and power, inviting his disciples to participate in the miraculous feedings. How might Jesus be inviting you to join him in a life of compassionate service? As Mother Teresa reminds us, "If you can't feed a hundred people, then feed just one."[3]

In the Transfiguration, Jesus offered his three most trusted disciples a "sneak preview" of how God would exalt him at the Resurrection. Jesus' entire life revealed God's glory. What might it mean for you, borrowing a phrase from poet and novelist Wendell Berry, to live in such a way that you "practice resurrection"?[4] We are people who need to hold on to a kind of faith that still believes in the miraculous, both in big and small ways. The world is far from perfect. Sometimes evil can only be defeated with extraordinary good.

Take some time to think about and pray about how God is inviting and challenging you to a deeper faith.

---

[1] The J. B. Phillips translation comes closest to this literal meaning, "intending to come alongside them."

[2] From *Mark 1–8*, by Joel Marcus, in **The Anchor Bible** (Doubleday, 2000); page 432.

[3] From http://www.brainyquote.com/quotes/authors/m/mother_teresa.html. (10-6-10)

[4] From "Manifesto: The Mad Farmer Liberation Front," by Wendell Berry, in *Reclaiming Politics*, Fall/Winter 1991 (Copyright © 1991, 1996 by Context Institute); page 62.

4.

Teachings and Parables to the Chosen

Mark 4:10-12; 6:6b-13; 7:17-23; 8:14-21; 8:27-30; 9:30-37; 10:10-12; 10:23-31; 10:32-34

Claim Your Story

Do you recognize the name Randy Pausch? He was a popular computer science professor at Carnegie Mellon University. In September 2006 he was diagnosed with terminal pancreatic cancer. A year later he delivered "The Last Lecture"—about the importance of pursuing and achieving our dreams—to an enthusiastic audience of his students, colleagues, and friends. The video of the speech became an Internet sensation and was expanded into a best-selling book. Pausch was obviously an extraordinary teacher who attracted bright and devoted students, eager to absorb what he had to offer.

You can probably recall a gifted teacher who made a difference in your life, someone whose insight and wisdom you recognized as truth. The disciples close to Jesus encountered in him the gifted teacher *par excellence*. He said things to them that he did not say to others. Sometimes his disciples found the message empowering, sometimes they found it hard and challenging, and sometimes they were puzzled by it. What do you make of Jesus' teaching? How do *you* respond?

Enter the Bible Story

Early Teachings

Jesus provided personal instruction to his disciples partly because "the secret of God's kingdom" had already been given to them (Mark 4:11).

Private explanation for the disciples, like at 4:10-20, was a regular practice of Jesus (see 7:17; 9:28; 9:33; 10:10). This was helpful for the disciples; equally important, it is very informative for later readers. The fact that Jesus had to explain these parables to the disciples hints at the challenges involved in understanding these "simple" stories. If Jesus' closest followers needed explanation, these stories were not as clear as some interpreters might suggest.

In Mark 4:11, the word that the CEB and the NRSV translate as "secret" comes from the Greek word *musterion*, which is the only occurrence of this Greek word in Mark's Gospel. Here, the King James Version's translation "mystery" is to be preferred. The term "secret" confines the meaning of Jesus' words to providing a punch line to the parable, like a solution to a riddle. But *musterion* was a broader concept that implied that Jesus had provided more than secret information regarding one story. Mystery was the insight into what God's reign meant and how this reign occurred. Such insight into God's plan had already been provided for Jesus' "insiders." They were well on their way, since they were already following him. "Outsiders," however, received simple, but not simplistic, parables.

A few short chapters after this private moment with his disciples, Jesus authorized a smaller group of his disciples for a short-term mission (Mark 6:6b-13). Just before Jesus commissioned his disciples, he was rejected by those who knew him best. The rejection at Jesus' hometown synagogue, however, did not hinder the mission for long. In fact, it may have given impetus to Jesus' decision to send out the Twelve on their first solo assignment. Such a mission was why Jesus had chosen "twelve" in Mark 3. Prior to this mission, the disciples had been in a kind of training camp. In Mark 4, Jesus taught about the nature of God's reign, providing private instruction for them (and for a larger group of disciples, "the people around Jesus, along with the Twelve" [4:10]). In Mark 5, Jesus performed liberating acts for them to witness. Finally, just before he sent them out, an unexpected rejection confronted the mission as a signal of what was to be expected in their work in the movement (6:11). Their covert operations on behalf of God's reign in the world would not be received kindly everywhere.

Their mission was quite specific. They were to continue the Jesus movement in *households*. We need to remember that these efforts to spread the Jesus movement occurred in small villages, not in twenty-first-century Western cities. Neither did all this occur in first-century synagogues, the obvious place for religious renewal. Of course, Jesus had his own successful activity in the homes surrounding the Sea of Galilee. Synagogues, with established religious traditions and authorities, were not always receptive to new ideas and activities that may have represented a new movement of God, however. So Jesus prepared his disciples for potential rejection. But wherever rejection existed, so would judgment: "Shake the dust off your feet" (Mark 6:11). In this case, the disciples' mission was successful (6:12-13). The disciples, who appeared clueless in several earlier incidents, apparently understood enough to carry out a mission effectively organized by Jesus.

About the Christian Faith

Early Christian Missionary Activity

Jesus' disciples proclaimed messages that sought repentance, they performed exorcisms, and they healed the sick (Mark 6:12-13). A few decades later, missionaries had other tasks that defined their activities. From Second John we learn that missionary teaching should advocate that "Jesus Christ came as a human being," otherwise the missionaries should not be welcomed into the house-church of that region of the country (2 John 7, 10). From the *Didache*, a late first-century Christian document, we discover that a teacher or apostle should be received in the same manner as a community would receive the Lord (11.4). But if that same prophet should stay longer than two days or if that teacher should say, even in the Spirit, "Give me money," then he was a "false prophet" (11.5, 6, 12).

However, just because one is involved in doing the right things does not guarantee that one will understand God's intentions. The disciples failed to understand Jesus' teaching again, this time following a debate

Jesus had with the Pharisees. The disciples' limited understanding was an ongoing theme in Mark's Gospel (see 4:13; 6:52). Once again they received a private audience (7:17) in a "house" and more details.

In Mark 7, Jesus was confronted by some religious leaders about the ritual of washing hands before eating. Mark's Jesus used this opportunity to talk about the broader concept of eating or not eating certain foods (7:14-23). Jesus' basic argument here was that nothing can physically enter a person and make him or her impure in God's sight. Rather, the things that are displeasing to God are the things that come from within, from within a heart that fails to recognize how personal choices can negatively affect many others. Jesus' explanation included a lesson in biology (7:18-19). He added a discussion on the place of origin of defilement: the heart (7:21). From the heart can stem evil, and evil brings dishonesty. This type of heart generates a selfish attitude that seeks to aggrandize one's own individual pleasures. The list of "pleasures" Jesus provided covers many of the significant areas that still define human relationships today: sex, money, pride, and jealousy. Indulgence in these areas—not what one eats or drinks—will often damage human relationships. The selfish things that come out of an unsettled heart, from inside our wandering minds, are still the things that disturb God the most.

Following the second miraculous feeding, Mark 8:14-21 reports that the disciples, who had forgotten to carry along bread—except for one loaf—went on another private boat ride. As we have recognized already, Jesus accomplished much by way of private teaching moments when in homes and in boats. In this teaching moment, bread once again was the main issue. Jesus chided the disciples for failing to remember that God had already provided the bread that was needed. The memory of all that God had done should prompt in the disciples (and in Mark's readers) renewed trust in God.

The miracles of Jesus can elicit faith; they do not demand faith. Jesus had offered the marks of the Kingdom repeatedly. Some folk never see the acts of God in their midst, even though they are right before their eyes. Cups of cold water given to strangers are powerful signs of God's ongoing

About the Scripture

Daily Bread

In addition to the symbolic implications of the two feeding stories, these stories were simply about how the mission of Jesus (and inevitably of his followers) was geared toward providing the basic necessities of life. It was no surprise, in a first-century context, that Jesus (in Matthew 6:11 and Luke 11:3) instructed his listeners to pray for the bread needed each day. Jesus prayed and acted in a manner that clearly expressed his concern for the basic needs of human existence. So should his followers!

activity among us. In fact, in the sequence provided here, it was seeing, hearing, and remembering that set up the challenge to the disciples (Mark 8:18). Yet, unlike the case with the Pharisees (in 8:11-12), Jesus reminded his hardheaded and hardhearted followers that plenty remained after the two feedings of the Jewish (Mark 6) and Gentile (Mark 8) crowds. The "leftovers" (8:19a) were significant: Jesus would provide more than was necessary. The numbers "Twelve" and "Seven" implied completeness (8:19b-20). Yet the final question in 8:21 remained unanswered by the disciples: "And you still don't understand?" The disciples were not unlike us, who frequently promote our own agendas—rather than God's—when it comes to, for example, dispersing the church's funds. What should we be expected to do for the mission of God? Do we not expect God to provide adequately?

Three Predictions of Jesus' Death and His Identity as Messiah

With his closest followers, Jesus tended to wrestle with his own identity out loud. This type of communal struggle was fitting in first-century society. For Jesus to make outlandish claims about himself ("I am God." or "I am the Son of God.") would cast public shame upon him in the honor/shame society of first-century life. What was more appropriate was for one's friends and family to acknowledge a person's elevated status. That seems to have been one of the main points of Jesus' question of his disciples, "Who do people say that I am?" (Mark 8:27). What were others starting to wonder about Jesus in light of his actions and teachings? Did these perceptions begin to spread among enough people to attract some of the large crowds Jesus was beginning to draw?

On three occasions, beginning with Jesus' private moment with the disciples in Caesarea Philippi, Jesus informed his closest followers about his upcoming death (Mark 8:31-32; 9:30-32; 10:32-34). Repeating the prediction of his death was not surprising given the continual portrayal of the disciples as oblivious. Such repetition also allowed the ancient (and the present) audience to recognize the significance of this message. Jesus wanted his audience to grasp the true nature of his messianic calling. He was not the great, militaristic Messiah who was coming to overthrow the political enemies of Israel. His message of the coming reign of God would not advocate taking up arms to fight Rome, despite common ancient expectations that this was what the coming Messiah would do. Furthermore, Jesus wanted followers who would also be willing to sacrifice power in order to carry out God's mission in the world: "All who lose their lives because of me . . . will save them" (8:35).

Comparing the three predictions, there are some subtle (and not so subtle) differences. Only in the first prediction was any disciple (Peter) bold enough to challenge Jesus: "Peter took hold of Jesus and, scolding him, began to correct him" (Mark 8:32). After the second prediction, the disciples asked nothing because of their overall fear (9:32). *Before* Jesus even offered the third prediction, the fear was mentioned again (10:32). While Jesus moved toward his death, some of his followers moved toward fear. Yet fear did not hinder them from thinking about power and status. In fact, they never stopped thinking about what access to the Messiah might mean for them. In one of these accounts, the other ten disciples grew upset with James and John, who were trying to work out a private deal with Jesus regarding their own future roles (see 10:35-39a, 41). These two disciples might have heard Jesus' talk about death (and losing power in order to gain), but they were primarily interested in situating themselves in higher positions of authority in the world to come. Many followers of Jesus continue to have a discussion like this in which they hear

Jesus discuss the kind of Messiah he is (that is, one who came to die), but it does not actually affect their own desires to be in the highest positions of authority.

Regardless of their fear—and despite the repeated forewarnings—James and John requested seats of honor when Jesus entered his "glory" (Mark 10:37). Their desire was for Jesus to grant "whatever we ask" (10:35). Jesus' metaphors of the "cup" (see 14:23, 36) and his "baptism" (10:38) both represent his coming death, about which the disciples seem to have been clueless. The idea that baptism served as a metaphor for death is not as clear in the Gospel narratives as it is in Romans: "Don't you know that all who were baptized into Christ Jesus were baptized into his death?" (Romans 6:3). Although there had been numerous predictions about the suffering Messiah, the disciples failed to comprehend the implications of such a leader for followers such as themselves. There is a radical, egalitarian spirit to following this type of leader. Yet Jesus' words in 9:35 and 10:31 fell on deaf ears.

Later Teachings for His Disciples

In addition to Jesus' descriptions of the kind of Messiah he had come to be, Jesus provided teaching to the disciples on the issues of divorce and remarriage and wealth. Both instances began with someone confronting Jesus on the topic at hand and ended with Jesus' private instruction to his close followers. After his debate with the Pharisees over the issue of divorce, Jesus had a private audience with the disciples (Mark 10:10-12). The disciples initiated this conversation, partly because the position of the Pharisees was the standard one of the day, following the teaching of Deuteronomy 24:1 on the permissibility of divorce.

Jesus, however, took his (more conservative) position on marriage even one step further. Earlier Mark's Jesus may have provided a more "liberal" interpretation of the law on "food" issues. But that was not to be the case on the issue of marriage. Divorce should not be an option, according to Jesus, because divorce *and* remarriage was equal to adultery for the one (whether male or female) initiating the divorce. Jesus interpreted the Mosaic command of Deuteronomy 24 in light of the Genesis account in an attempt to argue from the beginning of time. This teaching may seem harsh to us today, as it apparently did to Matthew's ancient audience as well. For Mark's Jesus, unlike for Matthew's, there was no exception clause that allowed filing for divorce. A person could remarry only if his/her spouse died (see Mark 12:18-27). For Mark's Jesus, unlike for Matthew's, there was also equal criticism of both genders, since either one could initiate a divorce (a rare practice for females, except occasionally in the Western part of the Mediterranean world). Among the Synoptic writers, only Mark acknowledged Jesus' extension of moral agency to women; but that meant they were then subject to Jesus' condemnation for making morally wrong decisions. The differences between Mark and Matthew on this teaching of Jesus' show how the early church also struggled with the "Jesus tradition" in an attempt to be faithful to what they thought he was saying.

This was not the last time the disciples sought further clarification. They were also troubled by Jesus' challenge to a wealthy man who seemed to be quite pious (Mark 10:17-27). In this story, a wealthy man confronted Jesus, asking a rather traditional Jewish question: "What must I do to obtain eternal life?" (10:17). Right after, Jesus used this confrontation as a teaching moment for his disciples. In fact, the next two sections, 10:23-27 and 10:28-31, provided further instruction to the disciples on Jesus' economic redistribution plan. This was not to be a "kingdom" for the powerful in society, an image we also see in Jesus' predictions of his death. Possessions were no longer to be viewed as immediate signs of being blessed by God, a traditional Jewish theological teaching that stretched far back into the wisdom tradition of the Old Testament. Indeed, the Book of Job was written (partly) as a response to this traditional theological conception. Although the disciples (represented by Peter's words) were themselves examples of recent followers who had left everything (10:28), they were disturbed by Jesus' difficult standards. From their perspective, no one would follow (that is, "be saved" [10:26]) if Jesus' teaching were to be accepted. But this was narrative irony because they had clearly followed. Jesus provided hope for their desperation after looking "at them carefully" (10:27), as he did the rich man (10:21). Sensing their astonishment,

Jesus acknowledged the overwhelming grace of God, with whom nothing was impossible. Indeed, Peter's confession in 10:28 was affirmation of God's possibility. True leaders, including those with financial power, must be willing to become "last" if they commit to the struggle of God's reign in the world (10:31; see also 9:35). In some contemporary circles of Christianity, this message of "blessing" has become distorted. It is difficult not to hear such a message on television evangelism that is so popular today. Yet the disciples' question was one that we all share. Do riches completely hinder one's participation in God's work in the world?

Live the Story

So, what did Jesus teach his closest followers? And what—among these teachings—is still central for contemporary Christians? Is any of it relevant for us?

Private instruction for the disciples reminds us of the need to be part of a church community. We need private instruction from one another and from our leaders who diligently search out the meaning of the Word of God. Bible reading must occur within safe, community contexts in which believers can engage and challenge one another's interpretations. The Spirit uses the Bible for such community development. Every person who participates in this type of experience will enhance their spiritual walk.

From the Gospel of Mark we learn that it is also crucial to wrestle with the meaning of Jesus' teaching on the kind of Messiah he was (8:31-32; 9:30-32; 10:32-34). If he was one who was willing to give up his power and his status for the sake of others, then what kind of followers should that make us? How hard it is to give up position, rank, and control for the sake of others. Yet this seems to be what Jesus calls the Christian community to do. Jesus' life was his "last lecture."

5.

Teachings and Parables to Those Eager to Hear

Mark 3:31-35; 4:1-34; 10:13-16; 10:17-22

Claim Your Story

Take a minute to recall a public speech that you have heard (live or recorded) that made an indelible impression on you. Was it Martin Luther King, Jr.'s "I Have a Dream" speech? Was it John F. Kennedy's Inaugural Address? Was it Maya Angelou's "On the Pulse of Morning" speech? Maybe it was Ronald Reagan's Brandenburg Gate Address. Or perhaps it was Ryne Sandberg's Baseball Hall of Fame Induction Address. Was it Oprah Winfrey's speech at the fifty-fourth EMMY Awards? Or was it Ursula LeGuin's famous "A Left-Handed Commencement Address"? Perhaps it was Barack Obama's Election Victory Speech in Chicago's Grant Park.

Whatever speech you remember, what about the speech or the speaker commanded your attention? What about the speech or the speaker intrigued or inspired or challenged you?

When Jesus spoke to large crowds, he commanded the attention of his listeners. Did he expect faith or trust in his message? Did he expect them to imagine a new way God was working in the world? Did he expect his audiences to live by his teachings? Did he tell these parables as a way of recruiting?

One thing is certain: The crowds would have a reaction when Jesus spoke to them. It was impossible to do otherwise. Jesus' stories forced some type of response from people. Sometimes the reactions were positive; sometimes they were negative. Why do you suppose the people reacted in the ways they did? What emotions do you suppose Jesus' words generated in those crowds? How would you have reacted had you been in the same situation?

Enter the Bible Story

Mark 3:31-35 is the first time in the Gospel of Mark that we read specific words that Jesus spoke to the crowds. Though the crowds were mentioned earlier in Mark's story (2:4, 13; 3:9, 20), it is not until the end of Chapter 3 that we know what Jesus actually said to them. And what Jesus said had to do with his sense of family. So we need to look carefully at the initial reaction of Jesus' family to his activity as reported in Mark 3:20-21.

What Family Meant to Jesus

In Mark 3:20-21, Jesus went home, presumably to Peter's house in Capernaum (see Mark 1:29; 2:1). But the crowds were growing so large (see 2:1; 3:9) that their presence disrupted normal activities, like eating meals. Jesus' own family had concluded that he was crazy, so they had arrived "to take control of him" (3:21). This harsh critique from Jesus' family has troubled many translators and interpreters for centuries. Matthew and Luke omit these verses altogether, and some ancient manuscripts of Mark follow suit. A few ancient scribes have altered the phrase for "family" in 3:21 to read, "The scribes and the rest" went out to restrain him. Many modern English translations have had trouble accepting this depiction of Jesus' family as well. For instance, the KJV and ASV translations have understood the Greek expression to mean "friends." But the Greek phrase, literally "those alongside him," was a common Greek idiom for family. Even the editors of the NRSV, who interpreted the idiom correctly as "family," lessened the tension between Jesus and his family by distancing his relatives from the accusation: "When his family heard it, they went out to restrain him, for people were saying, 'He has gone out of his mind.' " The Common English Bible, however, maintains the harsh reality of the Greek text (as does the NIV).

In an honor/shame society, Jesus' public actions would have threatened the entire family's status. The crowd, sensitive to the honor/shame culture, might have taken offense at Jesus' public disregard of his mother's wishes (Mark 3:31-33). When the Jerusalem representatives labeled him as an agent of "Beelzebul" (3:22), it was clear that things were getting out of hand. Can the family really be blamed?

As Mark reports in 3:35, for Jesus, "family" was anyone who "does God's will," who continues to fight against the dehumanizing forces of evil. Family consisted of those who engaged head-on the societal structures of deprivation that kept down others. "Family" was about liberation for the disenfranchised. The Markan Jesus was not antifamily; but a broader sociopolitical reality, the reign of God, had subsumed the local family unit. The new community would not be bound by racial, ethnic, or kinship lines. And the crowds were invited to participate.

Parables for the Crowds

Once Jesus had broadened his concept of the family to include those committed to the struggle for God's work in the world, he then provided his longest teaching segment of the entire Gospel of Mark (4:1-34).

In Mark 4:1-9, Jesus told a story about a common sower and his common seed. Jesus drew on the familiar experience of his listeners in this agrarian society. While the sower's economic status was not explicitly revealed, it was apparent that this sower at least had land on which to sow. The audience would assume that such a laborer would probably not be the landowner himself (compare 12:1-9). Wealthy landowners rarely worked their own lands. In addition, the manner in which this farmer sowed—that is, everywhere—may suggest a plot of land so small that it was necessary for a hopeful sower to sow everywhere. As Jesus' story continued, although a lot of seed was apparently wasted (4:4-7), some seed—supported by "the good soil"—was quite productive (4:8). The loss of seed, on which the majority of the parable concentrated, would have probably been a common occurrence for many in Jesus' audience. They would know about the loss of seed in life. On the other hand, the yield on positive production was unusually high, exaggerated to make a point (compare 4:30-32; 10:29-30). Jesus expected members of the audience not only to hear the story, but to listen to *and obey* the story (4:9).

Mark's narrative set up the parable of the sower as the dominant interpretive paradigm for understanding the following shorter parables on agrarian life. For instance, Jesus told another story about another sower, which deemphasized the human dimension again (Mark 4:26-29). This farmer was portrayed as one unskilled and uninformed about the dynamics of agricultural production. He was apparently a novice planter. He did not tend to his seed in the field but simply would sleep and awake, night and day. Surprisingly, he was even unaware of how the seed produced ("the farmer doesn't know how"; 4:27). Indeed, in this parable, the seed, and the Jesus movement it represented, grew "all by itself" (4:28) automatically (*automate*). According to Jesus, this is what the reign of God is like. There is one more significant difference in this parable. In this story, Jesus portrayed a harvest as well. The man eventually arrived in the fields with a "sickle" (4:29, NIV and NRSV), a term used only this once outside the Book of Revelation in the New Testament. The use of a sickle was an apparent allusion to Joel 3:13 (NIV and NRSV), which was set in the context of the coming judgment of God. The eschatological, end-time dimension of this story is more explicit in these later parables.

Jesus' next parable (Mark 4:30-32) used a "mustard seed" as the point of comparison to God's reign or the Jesus movement, a struggle that would become quite large in comparison to its modest beginning. Like in the previous parable, this seed apparently grew on its own as well. It was God's work! The salient allusion for understanding this particular metaphor came at the end of this parable: God's liberating reign would become large enough "that the birds in the sky are able to nest in its shade" (4:32). With the use of this image, Jesus intended another exaggeration. The "mustard seed," at its largest, could only become a great shrub (NRSV), a vegetable plant (CEB). Yet he portrayed the kind of plant that could house birds in its shade. Certainly, Jesus would have drawn a smile or two from his

Across the Testaments

Images of Comfort and Hope

Most striking among Jesus' allusions would have been the one to Ezekiel 17:22-24, in which the prophet also used hyperbolic language (see also Ezekiel 31:6; Daniel 4:12, 21):

> Thus says the Lord GOD:
> I myself will take a sprig from
> the lofty top of a cedar. . . .
> I will plant it,
> in order that it may produce boughs and bear fruit,
> and become a noble cedar. . . .
> In the shade of its branches will nest
> winged creatures of every kind. . . .
> I bring low the high tree,
> I make high the low tree. (NRSV)

Ezekiel's words were spoken to an exiled people, the people of Israel who had been captured and deported to the empire of Babylon. When they were at their lowest point, the prophet attempted to provide images of comfort and hope. These were the images that Jesus drew on for his own message about the way God rules in the world.

audience. This allusion would probably recall several scriptural passages (see Psalm 104:12; Ezekiel 31:6; Daniel 4:12, 21), all of which emphasized God's protection for the people of Israel. The development of God's rule would explode human notions of growth.

Mark wanted his readers to discern in these parables several insights about God's reign. The movement depended on good soil (Mark 4:1-8) but grew on its own accord without any assistance from those who sowed (4:26-29). Even the cultivation of such (good) soil did not seem to be within human capacity. Yet there was a human commitment to the struggle that Jesus discussed (4:24-25; there were sowers), and those who had been granted certain privileges needed to utilize those gifts. God's reign would surprise everyone in its ability to become much larger than expected from its origins (4:30-32).

Tension existed, in these stories, between divine and human activity. So it is with the struggle to live out the reign of God. God takes the initiative, but we have to respond. Sometimes the cares of the world and the desire for other things shift our focus away from God's desires for justice and peace in the world. Sometimes Satan distorts and detracts from that which has been planted deep within us. But there is hope in the power of the Word. Oftentimes, it will surprise us in the way it develops on its own.

Take Up Your Cross

In Mark 8:34, Jesus summoned the crowds for additional insight into his understanding of who he was and who his followers should be. Since he was one who came to suffer, true followers were those who did not ignore the struggle; they would "take up their cross." Such teaching had implications for the larger following and not just for the Twelve. But what was the meaning of denying one's self and taking up the cross in the first-century context of Jesus' day?

Jesus' teaching did not (and does not) mean "suffering for the sake of suffering" or the "redemptive value of suffering for itself." Womanist and feminist theologians rightly warn us against such supposedly "spiritual" notions, which are full of abusive potential. Rather, as the eminent twentieth-century preacher Howard Thurman suggested, one who follows Jesus "will choose rather to do the thing that is to him [or her] the maximum exposure to the love and therefore to the approval of God, rather than the thing that will save his [or her] own skin."[1]

In first-century culture, the cross represented a death reserved for slaves and state criminals. Only those who directly or indirectly challenged the imperial power of Rome were indicted with a death of crucifixion and forced to carry their own cross. So, to take up one's cross was a political statement. It implied that the bearer must live a life worthy of such a death. That is, the cross-bearer must be one who challenged the state or some other institution or authority when necessary; he or she must be one who was willing to suffer the consequences of living a life that engaged and encouraged those on the fringes of society. Herein lies life that takes up the cross. It is not a cross of individual suffering for the sake of one's own self-sacrifice. It is a cross that considers the other more highly than one considers one's self. This is living worthy of a cross; this is kingdom-movement living.

"Allow the Children to Come to Me"

In Mark 10:13-16, the crowds gained insight from Jesus' lesson about children. Surprisingly, the disciples attempted to stop people from bringing children to Jesus. Indeed, they "scolded them" (10:13). This was the common cultural reaction, but it was remarkable in light of Jesus' recent teaching on true leaders as those who welcomed such little ones (9:36-37). As they returned to common cultural practices, the disciples' forgetfulness continued . . . as does ours. After all, we live in a society in which, as Marian Wright Edelman says, "The state of millions of children in the richest most powerful democratic nation in the world is morally shameful, economically costly, and politically hypocritical." She then provides the following embarrassing statistics about children in the USA:[2]

- one is born into poverty every 43 seconds;
- one is reported abused or neglected every 11 seconds;
- one is born without health insurance every 60 seconds;
- one child or teenager is killed by a firearm every 2 hours and forty minutes;
- one child or teenager commits suicide every 5 hours.

Yet Jesus warned the disciples that those who received his mission and God's rule in the world must be willing to receive the children (Mark 10:15). Many interpret 10:15 as if Jesus said, "Whoever does not receive the kingdom of God the way a child receives it will not . . ." It is possible to understand "child" (*paidion*) as a subject. But the word order suggests that we should interpret *paidion* in the accusative case, that is, as a direct object. Jesus' words should then be understood as, "Whoever does not receive the kingdom of God the way one receives a child will not . . ." The latter would be more in line with Jesus' earlier teaching in 9:36-37.

Plus, the immediate context provided an example of what Jesus meant as he received (and blessed) the children (10:16). This was not about child-like faith (that is, humility; compare Matthew 18:3). Rather, to receive a child or to receive the Kingdom was to receive the other *and* to receive Jesus and the one who sent him (compare Mark 9:37). The reverse was also true. Not to receive children—the common cultural practice in antiquity—was not to receive the kingdom of God (that is, Jesus' mission). Receiving others was (and is!) key to the mission, as the disciples should have known (compare 6:11). Jesus expected hospitality toward children and others who were powerless in the same way that he imagined openness to the Kingdom.

An Obstacle to Accepting the Kingdom

In Mark 10:17-31, a rich man posed a question that no one in the story thus far had asked. It was a scene that confronted directly the relationship between status (that is, wealth as a sign of God's blessing) and following Jesus (10:17; compare 10:32-34). This confrontation was about "eternal life" (10:17; compare Matthew 25:31-46).

The Ten Commandments, according to Jesus, were a sufficient guide to eternal life for the honest seeker. Here Jesus listed those commandments related to human relationships characterized by justice toward one another, adding only "you shouldn't cheat" (Mark 10:19) to the list. Neither Matthew nor Luke (nor the Old Testament, for that matter) included the idea of cheating, which really signified the "withholding of pay" (*apostereō*). Despite the addition, the narrative provides no reason for readers to question the man's sincere claim to have kept the commandments since his youth.

Furthermore, it is also unclear why Jesus "loved" this man (Mark 10:21); but he did. Of course, we could claim that Jesus loved everyone he met. While that may be true, this is the only time Mark recorded that Jesus specifically loved anyone. Why? Was it the man's sincerity that Jesus saw as he "looked at him carefully"? Yet out of this love came Jesus' challenge: "Sell . . . and give." The man, like many people who face this challenge, was stunned and sorrowful; so he departed. Jesus' love for the man did not prevent Jesus from imposing a difficult challenge on him. As this story makes clear, wealth can hinder a commitment to Jesus' mission. Jesus did not state directly that wealth itself was the problem, but the desire to hold on to wealth for one's self was called into question. Redistribution of goods for the sake of the less fortunate was a sign of one's commitment to God's reign in the world.

Live the Story

The unnamed groups who were part of Jesus' audience rarely receive attention. Often the focus of attention—both scholarly and popular—is on Jesus' disciples or Jesus' religious opponents. Only rarely do we zero in on the larger group who heard Jesus: the crowds.

Yet most people in our society would be like this group, the unidentifiable, unnamed, unassuming crowds. They were very present in Jesus' teaching moments. Occasionally, Jesus even called them forward for a specific lesson, such as:

- God's reign is full of surprises.
- "All who want to come after me must say no to themselves, take up their cross, and follow me" (Mark 8:34).
- Those who are committed to God's work in the world are part of Jesus' family.
- Those who want to follow Jesus must welcome the vulnerable and the needy, whether children or adults.

Some who heard Jesus' message welcomed it as good news. Others were sorrowful when they learned the cost and turned away.

What is your response? What part of Jesus' message to the crowds do you welcome and embrace? What part of it seems a little—or maybe more than a little—scary? Take some time to meditate on Jesus' message to the crowds, knowing that he is speaking to you, too.

[1] From *The Creative Encounter*, by Howard Thurman (Friends United Press, 1954); page 123.
[2] From "Foreword," in *The State of America's Children*, by Marian Wright Edelman (Children's Defense Fund, 2002); page 6.

6.

Teachings and Parables to Those Who Opposed Jesus

Mark 6:1-6a; 7:1-13; 8:11-13; 10:2-9; 11:27–12:34

Claim Your Story

The intent of Jesus' parables was to challenge the religious sensibilities of his contemporaries regarding how God works in the world. But what about those who did not want to hear the teachings of Jesus? What about those who resented his teaching, viewing it more as a challenge to their own theological perceptions? Just as Jesus had followers (his disciples), there were groups of people who were opposed to Jesus in most every way.

Why did Jesus have any opposition at all? Wasn't he about doing good? Weren't the religious leaders also interested in doing good? More importantly, is it possible to understand the position of Jesus' opponents? Is it possible to articulate why these religious leaders would have had difficulty with Jesus without trivializing their position? That will be part of the challenge for us in this chapter.

Yet despite the tension with these religious representatives, Jesus did teach them. Why would Jesus go out of his way to teach, let alone talk to, those who opposed him? Could it have been Jesus' goal to create questions for his opponents in order to challenge their practices and views? How do we respond to those with whom we disagree? How do we respond to those with whom we disagree on religious matters?

Enter the Bible Story

From Mark 2:1–3:6, Jesus was in the middle of his first round of conflict with the religious leaders in the region. Very little teaching occurred, but there was a lot of tension. The conflict centered around Jesus' practices: (1) his authority to forgive sins (see 2:5-7)—an act that was reserved for God or God's priests; (2) the company he kept at meals (see 2:15-16); (3) the practice of fasting (see 2:18-20); and (4) what to do or not to do on the sabbath (see 2:23-28; 3:1-6). The tension from this section permeates the Gospel of Mark.

Rejection in Hometown Synagogue

In Mark 6:1-6a we learn of another group who opposed Jesus' mission: the folks in his hometown synagogue! Even the people who knew Jesus best were not persuaded by him. Do not get me wrong; they seemed to enjoy his teaching. Mark reported that they were "surprised" by the wisdom of his teaching (6:2).

On this occasion, however, the amazement immediately turned negative as a series of questions was raised about Jesus' family background. And they—hometown folk—seemed to know all too well about this topic. Their description of him, "the carpenter," "Mary's son" (Mark 6:3), ignored any mention of a father figure (compare Matthew 13:55). In first-century culture not mentioning a father figure would have been a direct insult on Jesus' character and honor, hinting at one who was conceived illegitimately (out of wedlock). This type of "biography," with a fatherless lineage, would have "repulsed" (from the Greek word *skandalidzo* [6:3], from which we derive "scandal") any first-century village. In this ancient society, Jesus was claiming to be more (that is, a prophet) than what had been granted to him through his family genes. That simply would not do.

Despite the tension and despite the lack of trust, Jesus still acted in helpful ways toward a few members of the synagogue. Throughout Mark's story, the author promoted faith as a critical element in the healing mission of Jesus. It is common to read "your faith has healed you" in this Gospel (see 5:34). But as this passage relates, faith was not always essential. Despite being "appalled by their disbelief," Jesus still healed a few people (6:5-6). God's freedom cannot be limited by what we think, believe, or do.

(Un)clean Hands, Food, and People

Once again religious representatives from Jerusalem returned to Jesus to question him about his disciples. Earlier it was about sabbath practices (see Mark 2:23-28). In Mark 7, it was about the washing of their hands. This was a reasonable concern; a few scenes ago the disciples were handling fish (6:32-44).

In Jesus' response to the Pharisees, he appropriated Scripture again. For him, Scripture trumped tradition. Isaiah provided the attack ("you hypocrites"; 7:6); Moses provided the direction (7:10).

By using Moses' teaching, Jesus argued against the tradition of *corban*, that is, a tradition that allowed one to devote all of one's means to religious causes. For Jesus, this tradition was directly opposed to the commandment to care for one's family. Financial support of parents was elevated over any "rules created by humans and handed down to you" (Mark 7:8). Economic care for the elderly was more fundamental than tithes for religious institutions.

About the Scripture

Jesus and the Pharisees

One reason that Mark described a lot of tension between Jesus and this Jewish sect known as the Pharisees and not other groups, like the Sadducees or the Zealots, was because this group held views similar to those of Jesus. Jesus believed in the supernatural (The Sadducees did not.), but did not believe in violent revolt against the Romans (The Zealots did.). The Pharisees, on the other hand, and Jesus shared several views. For example, both believed that the law was applicable to all of life. They differed, however, on how to appropriate it. Both believed in angels, demons, and rewards/punishments in the afterlife. Most importantly, both attempted to persuade the people that their ideas of God's work in the world was the more accurate portrayal of the Jewish faith.

The "rules handed down by the elders" (Mark 7:3, 5; "the tradition of the elders" in the NRSV) were distinctive to the Pharisaic sect of Judaism. These rules consisted of a long, oral tradition that was handed down generation to generation along with the tradition of the written Scripture. The former Pharisee, Paul, was one who was once "militant about the traditions of my ancestors" (Galatians 1:14).

Jesus' answer to the original question, about the disciples' lack of cleanliness (in Mark 7:5), did not come until 7:15: Nothing external can contaminate a person; only things that come from the inside can do so. Defilement does not stem from external things. This liberating word must have shocked the Jewish crowds and later Jewish readers. But Mark took it one step further in 7:19: All foods were declared clean. For Mark's own cross-cultural audience of Gentiles and Jews in Rome, such a declaration—much more "radical" than Matthew's version (see Matthew 15:16-20)—would have freed Gentiles to feel included in the table fellowship practices of early Christianity. Mark drew a liberating application from Jesus' controversy with the Pharisees and scribes.

A Challenge From the Temple Leadership

Following Jesus' symbolic action at the Temple (Mark 11:15-17), which was a primary factor leading to his death (see 11:18), the Temple leadership confronted Jesus about his actions (11:27-28). The issue of Jesus' "authority" has been a major part of Mark's story since the opening exorcism in the synagogue (see 1:21-28). Although readers have been clued in to Mark's acknowledgement of Jesus as "God's son" (1:1) from the beginning, the origins of Jesus' authority have not been clearly expressed to those people surrounding Jesus. Yet Jesus chose to respond only indirectly, posing a counterquestion about the origins of John's baptism (11:29-30). Jesus' opponents did not respond. These were politically sensitive leaders. They allowed the crowd's view to affect their own opinions and actions (11:31-33a).

Since Jesus' opponents failed to answer his question, he refused to answer theirs (Mark 11:33b). Nonetheless, his own question about the origins of John's baptism was an indirect response, especially since in

Mark, Jesus received his own baptism under John (see 1:9-11). Jesus' mission was intimately attached to John the Baptist's, which explains why the latter was such a prominent figure in all four Gospels. Indeed, recalling the divine approval at Jesus' baptism scene, readers know exactly from whom Jesus' authority came. All the events that followed this initial repartee stemmed from the Temple leadership in one way or another. Jesus was fully aware that the different representatives were all indirectly acting as agents on behalf of the main religious authority in Jerusalem.

A Prophetic Judgment Parable Against the Temple Leaders

The Temple leadership did not get off that easily. Jesus' longest parable since the parable of the sower in Mark 4 and the only parable he spoke after arriving in Jerusalem was a denunciation of the Temple leadership and flowed naturally from the tension in 11:27-33. The chapter division may hinder readers from recognizing that the audience to whom Jesus spoke in Mark 12:1-12 was still clearly the Temple leadership.

In Mark's account, Jesus' parable portrayed the owner of the vineyard as patient, almost to a fault, as he tolerated the killing of several slaves (12:5). Then without any signs of resolution, he decided to send his "son whom he loved dearly" (12:6), a clear allusion to Jesus (compare Mark 1:11; 9:7). In the parable proper, a rationale for sending the son was provided: "They will respect my son" (12:6). It would be common to assume that the presence of the son might have meant that the owner had died. The tenants mistakenly reasoned, however, that murdering the "heir" would allow them to claim the "inheritance" (12:7). The patient "Lord," according to the ending of the parable, would destroy these unfaithful tenants and deliver the vineyard to other tenants (12:9-11). In other words, as the Temple leaders grasped (12:12) and a comparison to Isaiah 5 clarified, Jesus condemned their care of the people of Israel, and, concurrently, their custody of the Temple (compare Mark 11:15-17). Unlike in Isaiah, in Jesus' parable the vineyard (that is, the people) was not destroyed; but the leaders were. Jesus was not, as some have thought, anti-Temple. He was not opposed to offering sacrifices at this holy site. What he opposed was the unethical manner in which these practices were carried out.

Across the Testaments

Allusion to Isaiah's "Vineyard"

While many scholars recognize an allusion to Isaiah 5, which provided a "love-song" about a "vineyard" (5:1, NRSV), such a connection was only implicit in Mark 12. In the Book of Isaiah, the vineyard was a metaphor for "the house of Israel" and "the people of Judah" (5:7), the northern and southern kingdoms of ancient Israel. In Isaiah's prophecy, the vineyard was destroyed (5:5). In a "benediction" preserved among the Dead Sea Scrolls, the "vineyard" was a metaphor for the "Temple." In light of that tradition, a number of interpreters connect Mark 12 to Jesus' earlier Temple action. If this link was intended in Mark's account, this would be further proof that Jesus' parable, as a link to his earlier Temple action, was a judgment against the leaders and not against the Temple itself.

Paying Taxes: God or Caesar?

The challenge from the Temple leadership continued throughout Mark 12, albeit in the guise of Pharisees and Herod's supporters (compare 3:6; 8:15). The involvement of Herod's supporters suggested where this group—as representative of the Temple leadership—stood on the issue of paying taxes to Caesar. Herod and his appointed heirs, his three sons, maintained strong, viable relationships with Rome, under whose authority they ruled. For these supporters, then, paying taxes was a simple matter. While individual Pharisees may have opposed taxation laws occasionally, Mark depicted a unified front here, representing a Temple leadership in favor of paying taxes in order to maintain Roman favor.

Recognizing their "deceit" (Mark 12:15)—"hypocrisy" in the NRSV (The Greek word, *hupokrisis*, means "an actor.")—Jesus answered their question in 12:14 quite directly: Pay taxes! And Jesus added a theological component: "Give to Caesar what belongs to Caesar and to God what belongs to God" (12:17a), which may have had political ramifications. What happened when Caesar's policies opposed God's or vice versa? World history generally, and US history in particular, is filled with examples of this tension, from black and white abolitionists in the antebellum period to women's suffrage to civil rights legislation. Yet in the narrative before us, the question was never asked, leaving a certain ambiguity. Just before Mark's Gospel was written, as the Roman-Jewish war began in A.D. 66, the rebels burned debt records in Jerusalem. But this was the action of rebels. How many average Jews thought that the tax percentages were too heavy? That is difficult to determine. Whatever Jesus meant—and scholars are divided on this one—the "wonder" (12:17b) the Temple representatives felt may suggest that Jesus' statement was more favorably received by them (for the cause of paying taxes?) than some scholars allow.

For some interpreters, this incident was a distinctive moment in Jesus' mission. It was, for them, the first (and only) time Jesus engaged in a broader sociopolitical discussion. But such an assessment can only be offered if one separates religion from politics, as modern Western societies attempt to do. The mantra "separation of church and state" is not applicable to ancient society. There was no separation for Mark's Jesus. This scene was part of a larger discussion that began with Jesus' opening message: "Here comes God's kingdom!" (Mark 1:15). Whenever Jesus raised the issue of God's reign, as he did in his parables (that is, words of the Kingdom) and in his exorcisms (that is, signs of the Kingdom), the issue was political. Jesus' entire mission was about implications for human, earthly life; life within community; living with others in a new community of followers of Jesus; living in a society in which God's reign was at the forefront of the community's actions.

The Sadducees and the Resurrection

Mark 12:18-27 reports the first and only appearance of the Sadducees in the Gospel of Mark. The Sadducees, the aristocracy in Jesus' day, were the Jewish sect most firmly attached to the stability of the Temple; so Jesus' action in the Temple also precipitated this confrontation.

The scenario the Sadducees raised about who would still be married to the spouse in the afterlife was hypothetical for them, as Mark informed us that this group did *not* believe in the afterlife. The Sadducees were in the minority with regard to a belief in resurrection. Many Jews, including most Pharisees, believed in the general resurrection (see Acts 23:8). Perhaps the Sadducees simply wanted to preserve the idea of a perpetual patriarchal system in order to maintain control in their present position. Otherwise, their issue was (really) hypothetical because they did not believe in life after death; so it was simply a game of legal meandering which Jesus played (he, too, cited scriptural texts) and did not play (by charging them with doubting the power of God).

Not citing any supporting text, Jesus claimed that no marriage certificates would be reviewed in the afterlife because humans would all be "like God's angels" (Mark 12:25), that is, spirit beings without marriage potential. In one way, Jesus' response was a liberating word for females, who would no longer be considered marital possessions. Then Jesus turned to the issue of resurrection, an issue that the Sadducees had not raised directly. Jesus, the charismatic prophet, distinguished his position on God's miraculous power from the Sadducees' position, laying out an important theological principle of life and freedom (12:24-27). The phrase "God's power" (12:24) occurs only this once in Mark; it is a key to understanding how to interpret Scripture within the Markan narrative. Jesus interprets Scripture, not woodenly, but in light of God's power to maintain covenant relationships with his people, even relationships that appear to have been ruptured by death. To deny the resurrection, as the Sadducees did, was to deny God's power to save.

A Scribe Not Far From the Kingdom

A Temple scribe overheard the debate between Jesus and the Sadducees and acknowledged Jesus' correct response (Mark 12:28). He, too, was probably a believer in the resurrection (that is, a scribe from the party of the Pharisees). His own question was a different one, one more fundamental than hypothetical. It was common, in the first century, for Jews to discuss and debate which commandment was the most important one (compare Mark 10:17, 19). Jesus' response drew, once again, on scriptural traditions, citing Deuteronomy 6:4-5—the standard daily Jewish prayer—and Leviticus 19:18. The addition of "love your neighbor as yourself" (Mark 12:31) provided Jesus' theological understanding that love for God was elucidated most expressively in love for others.

The scribe agreed with Jesus (Mark 12:32)! We witness a striking moment in which Jesus and a scribe concurred on a fundamental belief. In fact, the scribe went one step further by adding that what Jesus advocated here was "more important than all kinds of burnt offerings and sacrifices" (12:33), a conclusion, in this context, that was an implicit critique of Temple practices (compare Hosea 6:6). Jesus positively acknowledged the scribe's own well-spoken assessment by saying, "You aren't far from God's kingdom" (Mark 12:34). It was quite an appraisal. But why did Jesus not invite this scribe into the circle of God's reign completely? Was it his association with the Temple leaders? Mark, as he did so often, left us with another gap in the story.

Live the Story

We may find it difficult to focus on the stories that relate to Jesus' opponents because none of us really consider ourselves to be opponents of Jesus. In addition, few, if any, of us think of ourselves as religious leaders in any direct, influential (and political) way who might find in Jesus a rival for the attention of the people. Yet that was how his opponents saw him; that was how they saw themselves. He was an upstart, and because of that he needed to be stopped. So they did their religious and political duty.

For us, Jesus was a prophet and a reformer and even more. He was (and is) the chief agent of God, the Messiah. So we are inclined to see the opposition to him, as portrayed in Mark's Gospel, as opposition to God.

The challenge of these stories and this chapter is to slow down and think reflectively about how these religious leaders really do represent us in some ways. That is the challenge with which I want to leave us. Which of Jesus' teachings—his view of the religious leadership, paying taxes, the resurrection of the dead, or the greatest commandment—disturbs us most? What was it about the newness he wanted to bring to the world that most confronts our traditions, our religious rituals, and our practices? And yet, why do we place our most cherished hopes in that same newness of life that he brings and we desire for our lives and our communities?

May God bring that type of imaginative newness to us again in the midst of our settled and comfortable lives! Amen!

Jesus' Passion and Crucifixion

Mark 14–15

Claim Your Story

So much has been written and spoken about the passion of Jesus—and for good reason! To historic Christianity, Jesus' death is one of the most central elements—if not *the* most central element—within Christian faith. Christians today ponder (and Christians in every age have pondered) the meaning of Jesus' death. Did Jesus have to die? Why did Jesus die? Did he accomplish something by his death? If so, what was it? Does the fact that he died by crucifixion have any significance? What could it indicate? How has his suffering and death affected you and those close to you today?

Why did God allow Jesus to suffer such an ignominious death? What does Jesus' death say to you about sacrifice? Was it God's sacrifice? Was it Jesus' sacrifice? What does that sacrifice mean for your life today? Are you, as a Christian, expected to sacrifice as well? What do you sacrifice, if anything, in your Christian walk? Let's consider what guidance the Gospel of Mark offers on these matters.

Enter the Bible Story

Jesus tried to prepare the disciples for his impending death. He informed them on three different occasions about what was coming (Mark 8:31-33; 9:30-32; 10:32-34). If that was not sufficient, he also talked to them further about this death at what Christians traditionally call the "Last Supper" (14:12-26). His death should not have come as a surprise to them.

A Woman Prepared Jesus for Burial

It was time for the Passover feast, a time when Palestinian and diasporan Jews would commemorate the release of their ancestors from bondage in Egypt. Jesus may well have come to Jerusalem prior to this occasion, as depicted in the Fourth Gospel, to celebrate the feasts. But in Mark's Gospel, there was only one visit. And Jesus had come to die. In Mark's story, this was not a time of celebration. Others were not celebrating either. Instead, "the chief priests and legal experts" (Mark 14:1) were plotting the death of Jesus because of the disturbance he created in the Temple area. But the Passover festival deterred them, that is, until Judas' visit!

Sandwiched between their scheme and Judas' consultation with them was Mark's depiction of an unnamed woman's anointing of Jesus' head (14:3-9). This person arrived on the scene with no name and the wrong gender. Culturally, the public appearance of a woman without a male figure to whom she was attached would have been an act of shame. Her presence at the dinner table, however, did not shame Jesus or others, who were dining with a former (we presume) leper. While Jesus may not have been fully aware of the scheme that surrounded him, he was aware of the nearness of his death and interpreted this woman's action in this vein. Her act was prescient. Mark does not say how she knew it was time to prepare Jesus' body for burial. There is no mention of angels visiting her or of a voice from heaven speaking to her. There were no local village priests who forewarned her. Rather, in Jesus' words, "She has done what she could" (14:8).

In addition to comparing this anointing woman to Simon (Jesus' host), Mark's narrative encouraged his audience to compare her to Judas. While this unnamed female stranger committed this faithful act, Judas—Jesus' own disciple—committed the most faithless act of the story. No clear rationale is given. Many have suggested finances to be the prompting cause, as in Matthew's Gospel; and this may be as good a response as any in light of the complaints regarding the expense of the ointment. If correct, this was another point of comparison between the woman guest, who considered no expense too great for this preparation, and a disciple, who negotiated a payoff.

As for Jesus' statement about the poor (Mark 14:7), it should not be interpreted as an excuse not to do any good for the less fortunate (compare 10:17-22). But assisting the poor should not be an excuse not to do good for Jesus.

The Final Meal With the Disciples

From one meal to another, the celebration was filled with meals of remembrance. Of course, in Christian tradition, this final meal (the Lord's Supper, the Eucharist, Holy Communion) that Jesus shared with his disciples was the most significant in a gospel story that was filled with meals.

Two interrelated significant events occurred at this session. First, Jesus predicted the act of treachery. By the time the final supper occurred, readers have already been informed of the betrayer's activity. Judas had consulted with the chief priests who were very pleased to have his cooperation because they wanted Jesus killed (see Mark 14:1). It is the author's tool of narrative irony; readers know things that characters in the story do not. Second, Jesus provided a mystical interpretation of the bread and the wine,

Across the Testaments

"I Will Hit the Shepherd."

After the meal had ended, they sang a hymn. Then they took a walk, and Jesus continued his predictions about his disciples' failure. Jesus had predicted Judas' betrayal first (without naming names) during the meal (Mark 14:18); on the walk, he foretold the betrayal of the others (14:27a). For Jesus, the scattering of the disciples, "I will hit the shepherd, and the sheep will go off in all directions" (14:27b), had scriptural support, citing Zechariah 13:7. One element that received no further elaboration was the subject of the main verb. Who would "hit the shepherd"? As in the Book of Zechariah, the subject of the action in Jesus' words was God. If Jesus was the "shepherd" and the disciples were the "sheep," then God must be the subject of the main action. Jesus expressed no dualism here. God caused Jesus' death (that is, "I will hit the shepherd.") and scattered the disciples. But God would also raise Jesus from the dead (Mark 14:28).

relating them to his body and blood respectively. What was clear was that this Passover meal included a statement about a new covenant. The Twelve did not question its implications. Jesus connected his language about the end (in Mark 13) with his death. Again, for Mark, Jesus' awareness of the end was evident.

Jesus' Prayer: "Take This Cup of Suffering Away."

The uniqueness of Gethsemane ought not to be overlooked. Generally, Mark did not depict Jesus as struggling with the realization that his mission would lead to his death. Yet just before his death, the Gospel authors—with the exception of John—included this agonizing scene. Jesus felt the psychological turmoil of (expected) physical suffering. Mark displayed Jesus' personal struggle in prayer before a privileged group of disciples. Only the same disciples who witnessed the Transfiguration (compare Mark 9:2-8), which was a mystical alteration of reality, may have been able to handle the darkest moments of Jesus' emotional pain. Yet Gethsemane provided not only penetrating insight into Jesus' struggle but also another opportunity to observe the inattentiveness of the disciples. Their exhaustion from following Jesus had taken its toll (14:37, 40). Their failure here would foreshadow their upcoming departure, as Jesus predicted (14:27).

Then, before we are able to wrap our minds around the disciples' inability to grasp that their comfort and community were needed, Judas appeared on the scene for the final act of disloyalty (Mark 14:42-52).

Jesus' Trials Before the Sanhedrin, the High Priest, and Pilate

The trial of Jesus began in front of the Sanhedrin, a group of Pharisees, Sadducees, lawyers, and elders whose primary task in the first century was to adjudicate the affairs surrounding the Temple. These people were the religious and political powerbrokers in Jerusalem, the Jewish elite. As we are told, they were unable to locate proper witnesses to Jesus' actions in the Temple area (Mark 14:55). That is, they could not find two who could agree. So, as Mark stressed, only false witnesses came forward (14:56). The one charge that Mark reported was that some claimed that Jesus said that he would destroy the Temple and rebuild it in three days. But Mark's Jesus never made such a claim about the destruction of the Temple (compare John 2:19-21).

Finally, the high priest requested Jesus' response to the false charges (Mark 14:60). Jesus remained silent. Then the high priest asked Jesus directly whether he was the Messiah (14:61). Only in Mark's narrative was Jesus' response so clear: "I am" (14:62). It was the clearest Jesus had spoken about his identity in the entire narrative. The priest's reaction, tearing his clothes, was a sign of alarm and distress. The priest charged Jesus with blasphemy, that is, claiming a prerogative that only belonged to God. But, in actuality, Jesus had identified himself as the Messiah, an expected figure of the end times, though not one to be equated with God in Jewish theology. Yet the charge of blasphemy was assigned anyway.

While the Sanhedrin had condemned Jesus to death (Mark 14:64), their trumped-up charges were insufficient accusations for a death sentence. So they led Jesus to Pilate, the Roman governor and highest ranking Roman official in the territory. Mark offered no introduction for Pilate, assuming that his Roman Christian readers knew who he was.

The initial meeting between Jesus and Pilate was a brief "trial" surrounding one primary issue: whether Jesus considered himself to be "the king of the Jews" (Mark 15:2). On the one hand, Jesus did not deny Pilate's assessment; on the other hand, Pilate apparently did not find the claim to be worthy of death, blasphemy (a Jewish religious charge) or not. From Pilate's perspective, in the Markan account Jesus' death was the result of tension with the priests (that is, their "jealousy"; 15:10). It was a struggle between religious figures. Yet, politically sensitive to the crowd's reaction, Pilate still condemned Jesus to death (15:15).

The Significance of Jesus' Crucifixion

Death by crucifixion was public and political. Crucifixion was reserved for state criminals, slaves, and deserters from the Roman army. We can assume, though Mark did not report it, that Jesus would have been classified as a nuisance to the Roman state (that is, a state criminal). Pilate, as noted above, wanted to please the crowds and forestall any riots, especially during the season of the Passover feast.

The political rationale for a Roman public crucifixion was to forestall any future criminal activity against the state. Part of the maintenance of the *Pax Romana* ("Peace of Rome") was the policy of public humiliation of opposing forces. Of course, such public expressions of persecution dishonored the individuals so punished and brought shame upon the individuals' families and communities.

That is just background information, however. Mark was interested in something more. Oftentimes, his descriptions alluded to biblical passages. The distribution of Jesus' clothes (Mark 15:24) was an allusion to Psalm 22:18, a verse that was part of an individual's lament. Jesus repeated the first verse of that same psalm (15:34). For the author Mark, Psalm 22 provided appropriate commentary on the details of Jesus' passion, explicit or not:

> All who see me make fun of me—
> they gape, shaking their heads.
> (Psalm 22:7)

The political nature of this death was evident throughout this section, from the formal charge ("The notice of the formal charge against him was written, 'The king of the Jews.' " [Mark 15:26].) to the final derision from his fellow dying sufferers. These two criminals—actual enemies of the state—chimed in with the crowds, the chief priests, and the legal experts who were contending that the true Messiah would be a political figure who could save himself and, in turn, save all the others. Mark's Christian readers would catch the irony. This was exactly what Jesus was doing. His method just did not look like the expected way to secure the protection and salvation of all of humanity.

Meaning of Jesus' Death in Mark's Story: It Is Not About the Blood

One of the challenges of watching Mel Gibson's popular (in some Christian circles a few years ago) cinematic depiction of Jesus' death, *The*

Passion of the Christ, was the heavy emphasis on Jesus' blood. From the scenes of brutality in which the face of Gibson's Jesus was hardly recognizable to the dramatic scene in which Mary soaked up as much blood as she could with her clothes, Gibson focused our attention on the loss of Jesus' blood. This is not the place to go into the historical origins of Gibson's themes, which derive from medieval Christianity. Rather, I raise this issue because of its obvious difference from the biblical record. The Gospel of Mark rarely mentions blood. In the most brutal scene in Jesus' suffering when the soldiers take him away after his sentencing (see 15:16-20), there was exchanging of clothes, a crown of thorns, salutes, and even striking him with a stick—all in an effort to mock him. The soldiers clearly wanted to dishonor Jesus. But there is no mention of blood! When reading Mark's account of Jesus' suffering, one can hardly even find the word *blood* in the Passion narrative (but see "my blood of the covenant" at the final supper in 14:24). Blood was not one of Mark's primary points of interest in his depiction of the most significant story in Christianity. But this did not mean that Mark did not find Jesus' death meaningful. Indeed, he did!

Jesus' Death and Its (Theological and Political) Effect

At 15:34, Mark described Jesus' most poignant cry. Although bystanders misunderstood his Aramaic (the language Jesus regularly spoke), thinking that he called Elijah for assistance, Jesus actually spoke the words of an ancient, biblical psalmist (Psalm 22:1), an individual who lamented his own isolation and abandonment. In the psalm, the lamenter wondered about God's absence in his own personal conflict. Yet, at the same time, the psalmist recalled God's faithfulness through past struggles. In an attempt to describe Jesus' final emotional and psychological torment, in addition to his physical suffering, Mark wanted his readers to imagine thoughts analogous to the psalmist's.

Yet there was more. It was not only later Christian theology that recognized significance in Jesus' death, though various theologies of the Atonement would find little support in Mark's narrative. Mark, too, was interested in this crucial moment in Jesus' mission. Jesus died not because he had to die; he died because that was the consequence of his prophetic mission. He died because his life, as a life lived by God, challenged the status quo of religious and political power systems. While the Gospel of Mark may not argue for the necessity of Jesus' suffering death for forgiveness of sins (in fact, he forgave sins while he was alive; see 2:5), the earliest story about Jesus' mission did depict three crucial events of hope surrounding Jesus' final, earthly breath.

The tearing of the veil (Mark 15:38) symbolized a new era in which sacred space would no longer be divided from the most holy place. Mark's narrative does not make clear whether hope for all nations (All people were now free to enter.) or judgment against Israel (God's Spirit departed from the holy place.) was the foremost meaning of this apocalyptic event. Perhaps both were intended. The second event immediately followed this torn-veil scene and may shed light upon its meaning as well.

The confession of the Roman centurion (Mark 15:39) was the first time any human had confessed Jesus as Son of God in Mark's narrative. This point cannot be overstated. With the veil torn, a non-Jew could see and confess precisely who Jesus was. Mark's Roman, Christian audience would have been pleased to hear that one of their own was the first to offer such a confession following Jesus' death.

The presence of the women disciples (Mark 15:40) concluded Mark's depiction of events of hope surrounding Jesus' final breath. These women—some named, most unnamed—provided examples of faithful, committed disciples from the beginning of Jesus' mission in Galilee. Unlike Jesus' chosen twelve male disciples, these women witnessed the death and would eventually witness the burial and the empty tomb. They were the ones responsible for passing on these initial events in the development of the earliest Christian tradition.

At the point of Jesus' final breath, visions for non-Jews (and for readers) became clearer; religious symbols were reorganized (and some destroyed); and gender inclusiveness received more prominence than anywhere else in the narrative. Jesus' death was the beginning of a revisioning of the status quo. Now all that was left was his return to life, but new life had certainly begun with his extraordinary and unjust death.

About the Christian Faith

Howard Thurman on the Meaning of Jesus' Death

Jesus' death, as depicted by Mark, will continue to confound contemporary theories of the Atonement. The mystic Howard Thurman stressed two meanings for the Crucifixion: "1) when Jesus cried out 'My God! My God! Why hast thou forsaken me?' he declared the need to feel God's presence in that moment of terrible pain and anguish. Jesus wanted to be certain that the source of his life (God) was as available in this cataclysmic moment as during the other times of his life. In this cry Jesus again confesses his dependence upon God. Good Friday is a sign that life must ultimately rest, not in comfort, but in 'commending our spirits' to God. And 2) rather than the crucifixion being a God initiated event to redeem humankind, it is the logic of what happens to love in the world. To give one's self to God does not assure success, prosperity, or popularity. Since the social order contains evil, and since evil works against community, love faces immense difficulties. Good Friday is a statement about the nature of society, and the fate of the disciple of Jesus."[1]

Live the Story

So, what does Jesus' death mean for us?

It means everything! It shows us the consequences of living in God's mission. Whoever we are, wherever we are, when we stand up for God's desire to bring change into our local and global communities, the proponents of the status quo will not sit by idly. So there will be consequences. Jesus' death and the way in which he lived his life are signs of hope to anyone who chooses "to do justice, love kindness, and walk humbly with . . . God" (Micah 6:8).

Like the woman who anointed Jesus' body for his death, perhaps God will say about each one of us, "She has done what she could" (Mark 14:8). Thankfully for our sakes, "what she's done will also be told in memory of her" (14:9).

---

[1] From *The Mystic as Prophet*, by Luther E. Smith, Jr. (Friends United Press, 1991); page 69.

8.

Jesus' Burial and Resurrection

Mark 15:42–16:8 (compare 16:9-20)

Claim Your Story

When you think of a miracle, what comes to mind? Is Jesus' resurrection the pinnacle of all miracles? What does Jesus' resurrection signify? What would happen if you viewed history from the perspective of Jesus' empty tomb? What does this event mean to you?

Why didn't Jesus go into the public forum of Jerusalem after his resurrection? Would this not have been the best way to reveal that he had been resurrected from the dead and to show that he was the true Son of God? Why was this not the strategy? Why didn't Jesus approach his enemies to show that he had withstood their punishment? Why didn't he appear before the doubting public? Why did God not go public?

Instead, Mark wrote of women at an empty tomb. Did the women spoken to by the "young man" (Mark 16:5) understand the significance of the message they were asked to deliver? Why did God choose these women as messengers? Did they know that this mysterious individual was God's spokesperson?

It is certainly understandable that the women were afraid. How would you have reacted if an angelic being was telling you that Jesus had been raised? Would you have delivered his message or run away as they did?

Enter the Bible Story

Jesus' empty tomb changed the whole story. Of course, it was not as if Jesus had not forewarned the disciples that this would occur (see Mark 8:31; 9:31; 10:34). But Jesus' life and mission did not end with his death on the cross. In Mark's version, the story ended with an empty tomb.

The Burial of Jesus

In the Greco-Roman world, state criminals did not receive proper burials. Jewish tradition, however, stipulated the necessity of a proper burial even for criminals who had committed a crime punishable by death. Oddly, it was not one of Jesus' closest followers who requested his body for burial. Rather, it was Joseph, a prominent Jewish leader (Mark 15:43). Joseph had presumably met Jesus during Jesus' trial in front of the Sanhedrin (14:53-65), and he was one (presumably) of the council members who had condemned Jesus (14:64). In later tradition, Joseph would become known as "a disciple of Jesus" (Matthew 27:57; John 19:38), who had not voted to convict him (see Luke 23:51). He had come to perform the proper service for his teacher. But the idea that Joseph was a disciple was not part of Mark's story, which was the earliest record of Jesus' life, mission, and death. If Pilate had thought Joseph was a known follower of Jesus, Pilate would have been less willing to grant permission to Joseph to remove and bury the body.

Across the Testaments

Burial of Executed Criminals

Roman custom and Jewish custom were in sharp conflict over the handling of corpses of crucified criminals. For Rome, the punishment of crucifixion included the humiliation of being left on the cross for days, the body subject to decomposition and attacks from predatory birds. But for Jews, extended exposure of criminal corpses was prohibited (see Deuteronomy 21:22-23). Those convicted of serious offenses such as blasphemy and idolatry would not normally receive honorable burials, but they were not to be left unburied. The Book of Tobit, in the Greek version of the Old Testament, mentions burial of strangers as an act of courage and piety (Tobit 1:16-19). The Jewish historian Josephus reported to his pagan readers that Jews bury even their enemies.

Reading only Mark's account would have left his audience with questions, especially why "a prominent council member" (15:43) would have felt compelled to complete this pious act. In Mark's Gospel, Joseph appeared out of nowhere as a pious Jew who wished to ensure that the law (see Deuteronomy 21) was carried out. Perhaps the members of the Sanhedrin were responsible for the burials of those individuals they themselves had sentenced. According to Mark's account, Joseph's apparent kindness was done in haste. He failed to use the appropriate burial ointments. That omission would also be cleaned up in the later biblical tradition (see John 19:39-40). But failing to anoint Jesus' body left open an opportunity for the women disciples of Jesus who had witnessed his death (Mark 15:40). Two of them observed where Joseph had buried him (15:47). The women bought spices and returned the next day with the intent of providing Jesus' dead body with proper burial ointments (16:1).

Perhaps it was Joseph's anticipation of the coming kingdom that attracted him to Jesus for this final act. This may have been one more of Mark's examples of another person who was longing for God's kingdom but did not quite connect God's work to Jesus' mission. In an earlier example, Jesus had depicted a scribe as one "[not] far from God's kingdom" (Mark 12:34); so now another religious leader, a member of the council that opposed Jesus' activities in the Temple and elsewhere, also expected a coming kingdom. Joseph was but one of many Jews who were anticipating God's coming reign during their lifetime. Or perhaps his return to bury Jesus was a signal of his own ambiguous feelings about his vote to sentence him. So as Joseph looked forward to God's kingdom, he wanted to maintain a sense of honor in every occasion. Joseph's act of piety would eventually revitalize his image in the later biblical tradition.

The Surprise Absence From the Tomb

The presence of Jesus' faithful, female disciples at the critical scene of Jesus' tomb site should cause us to reflect on the role of women in Jesus' mission in general. As we know from reading Mark's Gospel, Jesus had a large entourage in his travel group, which included "many other women who had come to Jerusalem with him" (15:41). In the broader tradition,

About the Christian Faith

The Burial of Jesus

The Gospel of Mark reports the burial of Jesus (15:42-47) following his death on a cross. Paul also reports that Jesus died and was buried (1 Corinthians 15:3-4). That Jesus died and was buried is an article of faith in both the Apostles' Creed and the Nicene Creed. The Gospel of Mark and the early church emphasized that Jesus truly died. The Resurrection was therefore genuine, not the mere resuscitation of a drugged or comatose victim.

the prophet from Galilee showed little or no reluctance when he came into public contact with women. For example, in his encounter with the Samaritan woman, a story unique to the Fourth Gospel, the disciples were "shocked that he was talking with a woman" (John 4:27). Though women were never called "disciples" or "apostles" specifically in the gospel tradition (compare Paul's reference to Junia; Romans 16:7), the Evangelists occasionally used technical discipleship verbs in association with women (for example, "to follow" [see Matthew 27:55; Mark 15:41; Luke 23:49] and "to serve/minister" [see Matthew 8:15; 27:55; Mark 1:31; Luke 4:39; 8:3; John 12:2]). Significantly, the women's presence at the empty tomb established their prominent role as the central agents for circulating the most significant message of Jesus' life: his resurrection. The lack of any negative response from Jesus toward women in the patriarchal culture of the first century provides a rationale for thinking more imaginatively about the possibilities that may have been present for women in the early Jesus movement that the tradition may have downplayed.

Now let's turn our attention more specifically to what happened at the tomb in Mark's account. Three faithful women—Mary Magdalene, Mary (the mother of James and Joses, not Jesus' mother), and Salome—witnessed Jesus' death on the cross (Mark 15:40) and, at least two of them, his burial (15:47). On the final day (of the story in Mark), they arrived to prepare the body with ointments. These spices would have assisted with the gradual decomposition of the body and reduced the stench of decay.

In Jewish tradition, one year after burial, family members would retrieve the bones of the deceased and move them to a final resting place.

The women were not as concerned about the condition of Jesus' body as they were about the large stone at the entrance of the tomb. But, to their pleasant surprise, the stone had been rolled away. Their amazement increased when a "young man" (Mark 16:5) spoke to them. Mark's human-like figure, dressed in an angelic "white robe" (16:5), exemplified the apocalyptic nature of this event.

As the women observed, the tomb was empty. Yet they were unable to speak. Instead, the final spoken words of Mark's story came from the mysterious "young man" who spoke on behalf of God. And he spoke words of hope: "He has been raised" (Mark 16:6). Jesus was planning to reunite with his disciples in Galilee, and these women were to pass along that message. The final words of the Gospel of Mark were words of regathering, reunion, and hope.

The Promised Regathering and Ending

So the women went and told the disciples everything this angelic being said—right!?! Not at all! Instead, their fear overwhelmed their speech; and the entire story of Mark's Gospel ended with the final words of alarm, "They said nothing to anyone, because they were afraid" (16:8). Of course, this was Mark, the storyteller, at work. The Evangelist was not writing simply to give straightforward information about Jesus' life and death. He did that, but there was more to his writing agenda. Mark was writing this story for a purpose. He wrote for believers who knew a part of the story already. One significant part they knew was that someone, one of these women, had to have told someone else. If not, then they themselves never would have heard. They would not have been gathered together in Christian community. They would not have been worshiping Jesus as God in their Roman house churches. They would not have been interested at all in a story like Mark's. And Mark would not have written this account either. But Mark's ending provided his original readers, and all subsequent readers, with a challenge. He did not need a "happy ending."

About the Scripture

Women as Witnesses to the Resurrection

Let me introduce one relevant example of how the early Christian tradition attempted to diminish the role of women in Jesus' mission: the witnesses to Jesus' resurrection. In First Corinthians, in a tradition that was handed on to Paul (15:3), Jesus *first* appeared to Cephas, *then* to the twelve disciples *before* appearing to a large number (more than five hundred) of brothers *and sisters* at once (15:5-6). But there was one point on which all four Gospels agree: The women were the *first persons* to witness Jesus' empty tomb and, in some cases, resurrection appearance (Matthew 28:1-10 ; Mark 16:1-8; Luke 24:1-12; John 20:1-18). Furthermore, only Luke reported that the women's announcement of this miracle was not believed at first (Luke 24:11; see also Mark 6:9-11, which is part of the longer ending of Mark added later). In the other Gospels, there was no reason to question the trustworthiness of the witnesses.

The greatest story ever told was also the most startling one. Jesus had been mocked, crucified, and buried; yet he was not found in his tomb. Since Jesus had died under the decisions of the primary political and religious authorities of his day, what would Mark's readers do with the story of his ongoing life and Spirit among them? Would it strengthen them against those sociopolitical powers? Equally important, what will we do?

What Is Missing From Mark's Ending

The ending of Mark's Gospel has been viewed as unusual from ancient times to the present. But this is more about our assumptions about how Mark's story should end than it is about any fault of the author, whose purposes were clear. If Mark's original story ended at 16:8, as most scholars think it did, the story omitted a number of key events that other Gospels recorded. In Mark's account, there was no resurrected body (though it was implied by the empty tomb), no reunion with the disciples (though a promise of one was given), no grand commissioning of the disciples, and no ascension of Jesus' body into heaven. Readers have to turn to the other Gospels for these events. Even then, each Gospel offered its own unique ending. For example, Jesus' ascension to heaven was only recorded in Luke's Gospel (24:50-51). These apparent omissions do help to explain why some ancient scribes thought it necessary to write additional endings to Mark's story.

The Longer Endings of the Gospel of Mark (16:9; 16:9-20)

In the history of early Christianity, a number of individual scribes also had difficulty with Mark's ending. Ending the story about Jesus with fear must have seemed inappropriate. How could the good news of Jesus Christ end with no one saying anything? Plus, other Gospel accounts appeared to have more "appropriate" endings. So at least two "endings" have become part of the published accounts of the Gospel of Mark. Most English translations include the "longer ending of Mark" (16:9-20), while some also include the "shorter ending of Mark" (16:9).

The "shorter ending," added no earlier than the fourth century, provided a much more direct link to the silence of Mark 16:8. The lack of a smooth transition notwithstanding, this ending suggested that the women eventually reported their experience to "those who were with Peter," after which the "message of eternal salvation" went out "from the east to the west," into the whole world (Mark 16:9). This ending resolved the problem of silence.

The "longer ending" was apparently not added to the Gospel until the middle of the second century. While its opening verse coincided with and probably depended on other Gospel accounts (see John 20:14-18), it did not flow neatly from 16:8. In fact, it seems not to flow at all! But this longer ending did resolve issues related to Jesus' bodily appearance, a commissioning, and Jesus' ascension. All subsequent attempts to end Mark's Gospel more suitably, however, have obscured the startling challenge of Mark's ending.

If the story ended at Mark 16:8, as most critical editions of the Greek New Testament suggest, then hope was not defined by a resurrection, that is, by a physical appearance of Jesus. Rather, Mark's message of hope was illustrated by an empty tomb and a promised regathering. That may mean that hope in this story was derived from the absence of Jesus and the bond

About the Scripture

Raised by God

The CEB and NRSV translation of Mark 16:6 ("He has been raised.") is much to be preferred to the rendering of the RSV and NIV ("He has risen."). The point here and throughout the New Testament is that Jesus did not rise automatically or of his own accord. Rather, he was raised by the action of God. This was a central message of the early Christians. In Peter's Pentecost Day sermon, he announced, "God raised him up! God freed him from death's dreadful grip, since it was impossible for death to hang on to him" (Acts 2:24; see also Romans 10:9; Galatians 1:1). The Resurrection was God's answer to the Crucifixion and the cry of dereliction in Mark 15:34. God did *not* abandon Jesus the Messiah!

of community among those relying on his promised return. It was a story of community. The "young man" in the empty tomb (who spoke as God's messenger) promised that Jesus would meet again with the disciples in Galilee, at the place where the mission began (Mark 16:5-7). It was a story about new beginnings in the absence of Jesus but in the presence of each other. This story—Mark's story, Jesus' story, God's story—was one that challenged any followers of Jesus to return to the beginnings of the mission and begin anew with the Spirit of Jesus in their midst. As these women fled from Jesus' tomb "with terror and dread" (16:8), so must all followers of Jesus leave the empty tomb and imagine what will be next in the mission of the Kingdom. More importantly, how will God use us to continue Jesus' mission, goals, and objectives that began in a small village in Galilee?

Live the Story

So, what does Jesus' empty tomb mean for us? What does his promise of meeting the disciples (and, us!) in Galilee mean to us? What might it mean for the presence of Jesus' Spirit to abide with us in the twenty-first century?

May we remember the Lord's resurrection every time newness breaks into our carefully constructed and controlled communities! May we remember the empty tomb every time we experience that sense of dread that the status quo of history is changing right before our eyes! May we remember that God's miraculous Spirit continues to cross boundaries of class, race, gender, and all other humanly erected divides!

As we gather in our respective faith communities, may we trust what God's messenger has spoken: "You will see him there, just as he told you." Amen.

Leader Guide

People often view the Bible as a maze of obscure people, places, and events from centuries ago and struggle to relate it to their daily lives. IMMERSION invites us to experience the Bible as a record of God's loving revelation to humankind. These studies recognize our emotional, spiritual, and intellectual needs and welcome us into the Bible story and into deeper faith.

As leader of an IMMERSION group, you will help participants to encounter the Word of God and the God of the Word that will lead to new creation in Christ. You do not have to be an expert to lead; in fact, you will participate with your group in listening to and applying God's life-transforming Word to your lives. You and your group will explore the building blocks of the Christian faith through key stories, people, ideas, and teachings in every book of the Bible. You will also explore the bridges and points of connection between the Old and New Testaments.

Choosing and Using the Bible

The central goal of IMMERSION is engaging the members of your group with the Bible in a way that informs their minds, forms their hearts, and transforms the way they live out their Christian faith. Participants will need this study book and a Bible. IMMERSION is an excellent accompaniment to the Common English Bible (CEB). It shares with the CEB four common aims: clarity of language, faith in the Bible's power to transform lives, the emotional expectation that people will find the love of God, and the rational expectation that people will find the knowledge of God.

Other recommended study Bibles include *The New Interpreter's Study Bible* (NRSV), *The New Oxford Annotated Study Bible* (NRSV), *The HarperCollins Study Bible* (NRSV), the *NIV and TNIV Study Bibles*, and the *Archaeological Study Bible* (NIV). Encourage participants to use more than one translation. *The Message: The Bible in Contemporary Language* is a modern paraphrase of the Bible, based on the original languages. Eugene H. Peterson has created a masterful presentation of the Scripture text, which is best used alongside rather than in place of the CEB or another primary English translation.

One of the most reliable interpreters of the Bible's meaning is the Bible itself. Invite participants first of all to allow Scripture to have its say. Pay attention to context. Ask questions of the text. Read every passage with curiosity, always seeking to answer the basic Who? What? Where? When? and Why? questions.

Bible study groups should also have handy essential reference resources in case someone wants more information or needs clarification on specific words, terms, concepts, places, or people mentioned in the Bible. A Bible dictionary, Bible atlas, concordance, and one-volume Bible commentary together make for a good, basic reference library.

The Leader's Role

An effective leader prepares ahead. This leader guide provides easy to follow, step-by-step suggestions for leading a group. The key task of the leader is to guide discussion and activities that will engage heart and head and will invite faith development. Discussion questions are included, and you may want to add questions posed by you or your group. Here are suggestions for helping your group engage Scripture:

State questions clearly and simply.

Ask questions that move Bible truths from "outside" (dealing with concepts, ideas, or information about a passage) to "inside" (relating to the experiences, hopes, and dreams of the participants).

Work for variety in your questions, including compare and contrast, information recall, motivation, connections, speculation, and evaluation.

Avoid questions that call for yes-or-no responses or answers that are obvious.

Don't be afraid of silence during a discussion. It often yields especially thoughtful comments.

Test questions before using them by attempting to answer them yourself.

When leading a discussion, pay attention to the mood of your group by "listening" with your eyes as well as your ears.

Guidelines for the Group

IMMERSION is designed to promote full engagement with the Bible for the purpose of growing faith and building up Christian community. While much can be gained from individual reading, a group Bible study offers an ideal setting in which to achieve these aims. Encourage participants to bring their Bibles and read from Scripture during the session. Invite participants to consider the following guidelines as they participate in the group:

Respect differences of interpretation and understanding.

Support one another with Christian kindness, compassion, and courtesy.

Listen to others with the goal of understanding rather than agreeing or disagreeing.

Celebrate the opportunity to grow in faith through Bible study.

Approach the Bible as a dialogue partner, open to the possibility of being challenged or changed by God's Word.

Recognize that each person brings unique and valuable life experiences to the group and is an important part of the community.

Reflect theologically—that is, be attentive to three basic questions: What does this say about God? What does this say about me/us? What does this say about the relationship between God and me/us?

Commit to a *lived faith response* in light of insights you gain from the Bible. In other words, what changes in attitudes (how you believe) or actions (how you behave) are called for by God's Word?

Group Sessions

The group sessions, like the chapters themselves, are built around three sections: "Claim Your Story," "Enter the Bible Story," and "Live the Story." Sessions are designed to move participants from an awareness of their own life story, issues, needs, and experiences into an encounter and dialogue with the story of Scripture and to make decisions integrating their personal stories and the Bible's story.

The session plans in the following pages will provide questions and activities to help your group focus on the particular content of each chapter. In addition to questions and activities, the plans will include chapter title, Scripture, and faith focus.

Here are things to keep in mind for all the sessions:

Prepare Ahead
Study the Scripture, comparing different translations and perhaps a paraphrase.
Read the chapter, and consider what it says about your life and the Scripture.
Gather materials such as large sheets of paper or a markerboard with markers.
Prepare the learning area. Write the faith focus for all to see.

Welcome Participants
Invite participants to greet one another.
Tell them to find one or two people and talk about the faith focus.
Ask: What words stand out for you? Why?

Guide the Session
Look together at "Claim Your Story." Ask participants to give their reactions to the stories and examples given in each chapter. Use questions from the session plan to elicit comments based on personal experiences and insights.

Ask participants to open their Bibles and "Enter the Bible Story." For each portion of Scripture, use questions from the session plan to help participants gain insight into the text and relate it to issues in their own lives.

Step through the activity or questions posed in "Live the Story." Encourage participants to embrace what they have learned and to apply it in their daily lives.

Invite participants to offer their responses or insights about the boxed material in "Across the Testaments," "About the Scripture," and "About the Christian Faith."

Close the Session
Encourage participants to read the following week's Scripture and chapter before the next session.
Offer a closing prayer.

1. Jesus' Authority as Son of God
Mark 1:1-20; 3:13-19

Faith Focus
Jesus' authority comes from God, a part of God's plan for the world. So, too, are we given authority as Jesus' disciples, through the power of the Spirit, to serve God in various ways.

Before the Session
As you prepare for the session, reflect on the authority Jesus grants us, through the work of the Holy Spirit, to serve God. Prepare three large sheets of paper. Print one of the following on each sheet: "Do as Jesus Does," "Say What Jesus Says," "Be Present With Jesus." Place each sheet, along with markers, on separate tables or post in three places around your learning space.

Claim Your Story
Invite participants to name persons or roles of authority that come to mind. List their responses on a large sheet of paper. Ask participants which roles or persons they considered authorities when they were children or young people. Has their understanding of authority changed? Discuss some of the questions cited by the writer of the study. Ask participants if they can recall persons who did surprising things purporting to be in the name of God, such as proposing to burn the Koran. Say that in this session the group will consider the authority of Jesus, the source of his authority, and what Scripture has to say about his authority.

Enter the Bible Story
The Connection to the Past
Call the attention of the group to the boxed material illustrating Mark's connection of the case for Jesus' authority with the Old Testament past. Ask participants to choose one of the following Old Testament Scriptures to look up: Exodus 23:20, Malachi 3:1, or Isaiah 40:3. Have a volunteer read aloud each of the verses. In what ways did the Essenes prepare? In what way does the writer of the study say both John's and Jesus' preparation differed? With which form of preparation—withdrawal from the world in prayer and study or engagement in its everyday affairs—do participants most resonate?

Baptism and the Authority of John
Ask volunteers to read aloud Matthew 3:13-17, Luke 3:15-22, and Mark 1:4-11. Then ask: How does Mark's account differ? Why do you think Mark was less reticent in his account than the later Gospel writers were? How did Jesus' association with John bolster his authority? Why does Mark indicate that only Jesus witnessed the indwelling of the Spirit at his baptism?

The Temptation

What does the group make of Mark's statement in Mark 1:12 that the Spirit forced Jesus into the wilderness? The study writer asserts that Jesus' own life is a perfect example of how some challenges come to us from God. How does the group respond to the idea that God will not test us beyond what we are capable of handling?

The Cost of Discipleship

Ask the group to imagine being at their workplace. Suddenly, Jesus appears and invites them to leave their work behind and follow him. What would be the consequences? What would be the challenges? The study writer cites the costs of choosing a career as an ordained minister in today's world, but what might be other costs inherent in choosing to be a disciple today? Can participants envision any circumstance in which they would need to choose discipleship over family responsibilities?

Jesus' Authority

The study writer observes that with authority comes responsibility, no less for Jesus' followers than for Jesus. How are we called to say what Jesus said? In what ways are we as disciples called to do what he did? The study also says that the statement "he appointed them to be with him" is unique to Mark's account. How are we called to be with Jesus and with others in the faith community?

Live the Story

The study writer says that we might view the specific responsibilities Jesus gave his disciples as different types of Christians within the faith community. These responsibilities might also be considered as three different aspects of discipleship. Call the attention of the group to the three large sheets of paper with these three responsibilities ("Do as Jesus Does," "Say What Jesus Says," "Be Present With Jesus"). Ask participants to jot down on each sheet ways disciples might live out these responsibilities. Then ask: Is there one of the responsibilities of discipleship that is the most prominent in your own life as a disciple? Is there one you would like to develop more fully in your life of faith? Which seems the most challenging for you? Which is the best fit?

Remind the group that Jesus, through the power of God's Spirit, gives us the authority to continue to serve in many ways. Close with a time of prayer, asking for the indwelling of God's Spirit in the life of each participant.

2. Jesus' Authority and Power Revealed in Healings
Mark 2:1-12; 3:1-6; 5:1-20; 5:21-43; 6:53-56; 7:24-30; 7:31-37;
8:22-26; 9:14-29; 10:46-52

Faith Focus
Through the stories of healing in Mark's Gospel, Jesus revealed his power and author-ity. As Jesus' disciples today, the Christian community is called to participate in God's active healing of the world's brokenness and to work for the inclusion of those who suffer.

Before the Session
What do you think is the relationship between faith and healing? Where, for you, is the point where the mysteries of God move past understanding? Either obtain a hymnal with the hymn "Wounded World That Cries for Healing" or "There Is a Balm in Gilead" or locate one of those hymns online.

Claim Your Story
Invite the group to reflect in silence on the questions posed by the writer of the study about times when they have experienced healing or when someone they know has been healed. Then ask participants to consider the questions about times they can recall when they themselves or other people did not experience the healing for which they hoped.

On a large sheet of paper, list the definition of healing in the study. Ask participants to name examples of physical, mental, or emotional healing. Where do you most sense the need for healing in your life? in the life of the community? in the faith community? In this session, the group will consider what the significance is of Jesus' healings.

Enter the Bible Story
Invite the group members to place themselves on a continuum with respect to the two outlying positions on healing laid out in the study. Designate one side of the room "Healings: A First-century Phenomenon" and the other side "Jesus' Healings: Essential Representations of the Continuing Vibrancy of the Christian Movement." Ask volunteers to explain why they placed themselves where they did. Ask the group to discuss these two out-lying positions using the following case studies:

A pastor blind since birth recalled hearing the story of the healing of the blind man and wondering why God would not heal him. What was wrong with him that he was still blind? Did he lack faith? How would you respond to this man?

The youth group is discussing a healing story from Mark's Gospel. One teenager scoffs, saying these biblical stories are a good example of why she finds Scripture of dubi-ous help. How could Jesus actually heal such debilitating maladies anyway? Or conversely, if we can no longer perform healings, doesn't that mean we don't have the faith of first-cen-tury Christians? What would you say to this young person?

Call the attention of the group to the assertion in the study that in the Gospels, heal-ings were about something more than the healings themselves. Ask the group to form smaller groups of three people each. In each group, assign one of the following sections in the study to a participant: "Healing and Social Isolation," "Healing and the Forgiveness of Sins," "Healing and Overcoming Ethnic and Social Boundaries." Ask that each person read the assigned section and the Scripture passages; then discuss together the following: What is the issue relevant to healing? What did you find surprising or disturbing? In what way were these healings about the individual? In what way were they about the community?

In the total group, compare the stories from John's Gospel to the healing stories in Mark. What is the relationship between illness and retribution in each Gospel? What is the relationship between faith and healing? What does this have to say about the sovereignty of God?

Live the Story

Like the friends of the paralyzed man, we have to be willing to have enough faith to shape our actions for the sake of others. What are situations in our contemporary context that seem so intractable that it is hard to imagine being able to act as healing agents? How do we respond in the face of these complex systemic issues?

UNICEF's message is that 22,000 children die each day from largely preventable causes. UNICEF's goal is to move that figure to zero. What is the role of us individually in working to reach that goal? Why is a communal response important? What is the role of the community, in particular the faith community, in reaching out to end the marginalization of those isolated by a modern stigmatizing disease like HIV/AIDS or a condition like bipolar disorder or a developmental disability?

Recall for the group the questions posed by the writer on pages 23-24 of this study. Enter into a time of prayer; and invite participants to name situations, people, and systems in need of God's healing. After each is voiced, ask the group to respond, "O God, deepen our faith and move us to touch the wounds of the world." If possible, close by singing "Wounded World That Cries for Justice" or "There Is a Balm in Gilead"; or read the words aloud as a closing prayer.

3. Jesus' Authority and Power Revealed in Nature Miracles
Mark 4:35-41; 6:30-44; 6:45-52; 8:1-10; 9:2-8

Faith Focus
Jesus' nature miracles were designed, not to initiate faith, but to increase the faith of his disciples. Like them, we can respond fearfully to evidence of his power or we can see these demonstrations of Jesus' authority, and those "miracles" in our own time, as an invitation to trust God more deeply.

Before the Session
On a large sheet of paper, print the two definitions of the word *miracle* included in the study. Also print "If _____, it would be a miracle." Visit your local library or go online to get a copy of Wendell Berry's poem "Manifesto: The Mad Farmer's Liberation."

Claim Your Story
Ask the group to respond to the prompt you posted, filling in the blank with whatever first comes to mind. Record the responses on a large sheet of paper. Then discuss which of the responses would typify the first or the second definition of the word. That is, which are about divine intervention and which are merely about an extremely unusual event? Briefly discuss the questions the writer poses in the study. How many actual miracles can members of the group recall hearing about or experiencing? How can we know if something is a miracle or simply lucky happenstance?

Enter the Bible Story
Jesus' Power and Authority Over Chaos
Ask participants to close their eyes and imagine themselves on a small vessel in the midst of a ferocious storm, and invite a volunteer to read aloud the verses from Psalm 107 in the study. The writer observes that this psalm might have come to the disciples' minds when they were caught in the vortex of the storm's power.

In the two accounts of Jesus and the storms, Jesus had been with the crowds immediately before. Yet as the writer points out, when Jesus demonstrated his authority over wind and waves, it was only those in his closest circle who were witnesses to what happened. Suggest to the group that they picture themselves in a fishing boat on the Sea of Galilee. Ask them to listen as you or volunteers read Mark 4:35-41 and then Mark 6:45-52. Discuss the following:

In your imagination, what was most terrifying about being out on the water in the storm? When have you experienced a chaotic, stormy life situation? What was the source of your desperation?

In the midst of chaos, have you felt a sense of abandonment, as if God had turned away from you? If so, why?

Why would Jesus send his disciples out into the storm? Has there ever been a time when you felt led by God to venture out in a certain direction, only to encounter rough seas? Have there been times when you expected Jesus to rescue you from the waves when, instead, he was alongside to accompany you? In the face of chaos, have you responded with insight or with fear? with a deepening of faith or with a hardening of heart? When, like the disciples, have you been clueless in the face of a demonstration of Jesus' power and authority?

Jesus' Power and Authority in Feeding Stories
Invite the group to look at the two feeding stories, Mark 6:30-44 and Mark 8:1-10. The writer of the study observes that Jesus' compassion for the crowd led him to use the resources the disciples possessed to feed the people. Yet there was no response from the people to these miracles. Why does the group think this was so? Why, in Mark 8:14-21, would the disciples forget the bread and yet be so oblivious to what had just taken place before their eyes?

The Transfiguration
The study writer asserts that no event in Mark equals the Transfiguration in terms of revealing Jesus' true identity. Ask for someone to name the two features of the Transfiguration (Jesus' dazzling apparel and the appearance of Moses and Elijah). In what ways did the appearance of Elijah and Moses serve as a clue to Jesus' identity? Are there times when the breaking in of new life is so threatening that people of faith respond by clinging too tightly to the familiarity of tradition? Why does revelation evoke such fear?

Live the Story
Remind the group that Jesus' nature miracles were not evangelistic tools but an invitation to those already on the journey of faith to deepen their faith and understanding. The study writer asks, "How might Jesus be inviting you to join him in a life of compassionate service" (page 31)? Is it enough to be compassionate and to respond to the immediate needs of one person or of one hundred, or does Jesus call us to act with justice to ameliorate the systems that keep people hungry?

If you were able to get a copy of Wendell Berry's poem "Manifesto: The Mad Farmer's Liberation," read it aloud for the group. What might it mean for us, as the writer says, to practice resurrection?

4. Teachings and Parables to the Chosen

Mark 4:10-12; 6:6b-13; 7:17-23; 8:14-21; 8:27-30; 9:30-37;
10:10-12; 10:23-31; 10:32-34

Faith Focus

In his teachings, Jesus continually revealed to his disciples the kind of Messiah he was called to be. Like the clueless twelve apostles, we prefer to cast Jesus Christ in the image that best fits our agendas, rather than in the one that calls us to a different kind of status.

Before the Session

Do an Internet search for Randy Pausch's "The Last Lecture." Download it onto your computer for viewing by the group. If your class is very large, you may want to make arrangements to plug the computer into a larger monitor. Participants will need paper and pens or pencils. Prepare two large sheets of paper with the heading "Wanted: Messiah."

Claim Your Story

Invite participants to name a gifted teacher who made a difference in their lives. Was this teacher empowering, identifying gifts you possess that no one else had recognized? How was this person challenging, encouraging you to develop discipline or pushing you to examine your assumptions more critically? Was the teaching rigorous? Was it creative?

If possible, view a brief portion of "The Last Lecture." What characteristics of a good teacher does Mr. Pausch exemplify? What would you imagine would have been the characteristics of Jesus' teaching?

Enter the Bible Story

Early Teachings

What is the difference between a secret and a mystery according to the study writer? Given the Twelve's experiences with Jesus, why does the group suppose they remained so clueless? What might have been the reasons that the mission on which they were sent was to small villages and households, not to the synagogues or the urban areas?

Ask the group to name some rules or rituals to which your congregation has traditionally adhered. Some of these may be clearly stated, such as who can serve as an usher; and others may be unspoken, like what kinds of meetings can take place in the church parlor. What would happen if a child administered the sacrament of Holy Communion or if an unbaptized person received the elements? Ask the group to name specific actions related to the list of "pleasures" Jesus named that have the potential to damage relationships in the church. Are there some rules and rituals that really do matter as much as these sins of the heart? If so, what are they?

Read aloud Mark 8:14-21. Invite participants to name what the disciples saw and heard in the two feeding stories. Remind them that the Lord's Supper points to the need to remember the redeeming acts of God in Jesus Christ. What are we called to remember from these feeding stories? What does the study writer say the baskets of leftovers signified?

What are we reminded to remember about the bounty of God that is available to us when we engage in God's mission?

Three Predictions of Death

Distribute paper and pens or pencils. Invite the group to generate two job descriptions for the Messiah that might have been posted in the first century. The first should describe characteristics of the leader Jews had traditionally longed and hoped for, the second the kind of Messiah Jesus was hinting he was. After a few minutes, head two large sheets of paper "Wanted: Messiah" and ask participants to generate two descriptions as a group.

Why does the writer of the study say, "While Jesus moved toward his death, some of his followers moved toward fear" (page 38)? What was so threatening? In the face of lesser crises like the diminishing of a company's influence or the decline of a mainline denomination's membership, why do so many people respond by trying to shore up or grab influence and power? Why do Jesus' metaphors of the cup and baptism fall on deaf ears?

Later Learnings for His Disciples

Jesus took issue with the Pharisees' position on divorce, taking the much stronger stance that remarriage after divorce was equally adultery for whichever spouse, husband or wife, initiated the divorce. What does the difference between Matthew's account and Mark's say about the struggle of the early church and its attempt to be faithful to Jesus' intent?

What was Jesus' economic redistribution plan? In what way did Jesus' teachings turn upside down the traditional Jewish position that possessions are signs of God's blessings? What do participants think about the issue of whether riches completely hinder one's participation in God's work in the world.

Live the Story

Invite the group members to make a list of aspects of status as well as of the possessions they value highly. Encourage them to be rigorously honest with themselves about what defines their own status and to prioritize the list from the least important to whatever they cherish the most. How difficult would it be to strip themselves of these aspects of status? Encourage them to take the list home as a "final exam" to test their response to Jesus' last lecture, his life.

5. Teachings and Parables to Those Eager to Hear
Mark 3:31-35; 4:1-34; 10:13-16; 10:17-22

Faith Focus
Jesus' speeches evoked responses from the unnamed persons in the crowds. Like them, we have the opportunity to listen to what God's realm is like and to respond.

Before the Session
Consider a speech that made an indelible impression on you, and be prepared to share your response with the group. Contact some participants in advance, and give them the same assignment. Also locate Lincoln's Gettysburg Address. Participants will need paper and pencils or pens.

Claim Your Story
Read or recite the Gettysburg Address. Why is this speech so memorable?

Share why the speech you chose had an impact on you, and ask others you contacted to share what speeches impressed them. Invite the group to imagine they are part of the crowds that were attracted to Jesus. What might have drawn people to listen? What emotions do you imagine Jesus' words engendered?

Enter the Bible Story
What Family Means to Jesus
Ask the group to consider how they would react if a young person departed from the family's norms and took a diametrically different path. Would they be concerned about what other people would think? How do they define family? Does family depend on blood relationships, or could family be those who are close regardless of blood ties?

The study writer observes that for Jesus, family consisted of those who engaged head-on the oppressive social structures. What does it mean that the reign of God has subsumed the family unit? What, then, would be the definition of "family values"?

Parables for the Crowd
For most groups, the parables related to agrarian life will need unpacking. Ask participants to pair up. Then assign to one person in each pair the parables about sowing and to the other the parable of the mustard seed. Ask participants to read the Scripture passages and the commentary in the study and then summarize the information for their partner. As a total group, discuss what each parable has to say about the reign of God. What is the tension between divine initiative and human response in the coming of God's reign? Ask the group to come up with contemporary metaphors that would parallel these parables.

Take Up Your Cross
How does the group respond to the quotation from Howard Thurman in the study? What are the pitfalls and possible consequences of suffering for the sake of suffering? How

does that differ from the kind of suffering involved in cross bearing? What is "kingdom-movement living" (page 49)?

"Do Not Hinder the Children"

Invite the participants to respond to the following: "In our contemporary context, children are . . ." Call their attention to the statistics in the study about children. Often our rhetoric about children in which we characterize them as our highest priority is not matched by the reality of the circumstances that affect far too many US children. Ask someone to read aloud Mark 10:13-16. This passage is often interpreted in a similarly sentimentalized way that masks the real meaning of what Jesus was trying to convey. What was the status of children in the first century?

Discuss what the study writer says about viewing children as the direct object, rather than the subject, of the passage. What does it mean to receive the Kingdom as we receive a child? In our own culture, what would it mean if we took seriously the mandate to bless *all* the children?

An Obstacle to Accepting the Kingdom

Ask someone to summarize the discussion in the previous session about the theology of blessing. Read Mark 10:17-31, noting that in Mark's account Jesus added "you shouldn't cheat" to the list of commandments related to human relationships. The study writer asserts that wealth can hinder a person's commitment to mission. Is the problem wealth itself or the desire to hold on to wealth? Could the same apply to the "stuff" we try to hold on to?

Live the Story

Distribute paper and pencils or pens, and invite participants to picture themselves in the crowd listening to Jesus tell one of the parables in this chapter of the study. Ask them to respond to the following:

"When I heard Jesus' words, I thought about . . ."
"I think Jesus is trying to say . . ."
"His words made me feel . . . and I think I will . . ."
Ask volunteers to share what they wrote.

6. Teachings and Parables to Those Who Opposed Jesus
Mark 6:1-6a; 7:1-13; 8:11-13; 10:2-9; 11:27–12:34

Faith Focus
Jesus posed a challenge to the theological perceptions of the religious leaders of his day. We, too, are challenged to reflect on the degree to which our rituals and practices reflect the power and authority of God.

Before the Session
On a large sheet of paper, write the following: "How do we respond to those with whom we disagree on religious matters?" Also write the four practices of Jesus named in the study.

Claim Your Story
Invite the group to respond to the question you posted. Do you ever have dialogue with those with whom you disagree on religion? In our highly polarized national context, many people avoid any such opportunities. How can we avoid trivializing the positions of those with whom we disagree? Ask the group to ponder how we might engage in such dialogue, rather than simply restating our beliefs for those we know agree with us.

Enter the Bible Story
Call the group members' attention to the four practices of Jesus that were at the center of the conflict. Ask them to respond with a show of hands to the practice that they think was likely to be the most problematic. Invite volunteers to say why they made the choice they did.

Rejection in the Hometown Synagogue
Jesus' pedigree got in his way in his own hometown. Ask participants if a longtime friend or family member has ever accused them of getting above themselves or forgetting where they came from. What is the intention behind such an accusation? Is "hometown boy makes good" always a good thing? What happens when who someone really is gets in the way of the expectations of the hometown?

Unclean Hands, Foods, People
Note for participants that in Jewish tradition, hand washing carried a different connotation than it does today. Jesus extended the discussion by insisting that Scripture trumped the "tradition of the elders" of *corban*. Are there times when tradition takes precedence over Scripture in our congregational life? Is it ever true that our financial contributions go to shore up the status quo in our churches at the expense of meeting the needs of vulnerable people? In what ways was it liberating for Mark's audience to understand that externals are not contaminating? How might it be liberating today to have the same understanding about the external trappings of our faith?

A Challenge From Temple Leadership and a Prophetic Judgment Parable

Invite the group to read silently Mark 11:15-17 and 27-33 and the related section of the study. The study writer explains that Jesus' mission was intimately related to John the Baptist's. What was Jesus' reason for responding to the Temple authorities by asking a question about John's authority? Why might this have been threatening to the authorities?

Ask the group to imagine they are Temple authorities. First have someone read Mark 11:15-17 aloud, then the parable in Mark 12:1-12. In the role of these authorities, how would this parable be heard?

Paying Taxes

The Temple authorities supported paying taxes in order to stay in the good graces of Rome. Unlike in our society, Mark's Jesus would not have separated religion and politics. Ask the group to consider Jesus' statement that one should give to the emperor what is the emperor's and to God what is God's. Why would the authorities have been amazed? In the light of the Jewish worldview, what belongs to God?

Hypotheticals and Fundamentals

Ask the group to discuss this puzzling passage of Scripture (Mark 12:18-27), addressing some of the following: Why would the Sadducees, who did not believe in the afterlife, pose such a hypothetical question? Do you agree that Jesus' response might be liberating for women? Why does the study say that the power of God is a key to understanding how to interpret Scripture? How does Jesus' response to the scribe who asked about the greatest commandment underscore the criticism he had been addressing to the authorities? Are there times when our rituals, like the Temple practices, are grounded in something other than love of neighbor?

Revisit the four practices of Jesus that were at the center of the conflict with the authorities. Do any of these practices emerge in one of the passages the group has been addressing in this session? If not, what were the underlying issues of contention for the Temple authorities?

Live the Story

A popular acronym, appearing on T-shirts and wristbands, is "WWJD": What Would Jesus Do? On a large sheet of paper, write "WWJS" (What Would Jesus Say?). Ask participants to reflect on the questions in the study that challenge us to think about how the Temple authorities really do represent us in some ways. Invite participants to name the traditions, rituals, or practices that exemplify those resemblances. What would Jesus say to us about those things?

7. Jesus' Passion and Crucifixion
Mark 14–15

Faith Focus
Jesus' death shows us the consequences of living in God's mission. The way he lived is a sign of hope to those who follow him.

Before the Session
On a large sheet of paper, draw a large cross. Provide participants with colored self-stick notes and pens. Make a chart on a large sheet of paper for recording the trials of Jesus with these columns: "Trial," "Who Adjudicated," "Charges," "Jesus' Response," "Evidence," "Outcome."

Claim Your Story
Invite participants to read over the questions in the study and choose one or more for which they personally might seek answers. Ask them to print the questions on separate colored self-stick notes and attach to the large sheet of paper. Read the posted questions aloud. These questions are attempts to grapple with what the study calls "one of the most central elements—if not *the* most central element—within Christian faith" (page 63).

Enter the Bible Story
Remind the group that in Chapter 4, the study writer states that "while Jesus moved toward his death, some of his followers moved toward fear" (page 38). Ask volunteers to read aloud Mark 8:31-33; 9:31-32; 10:32-34. Do the disciples seem clueless, fearful, in denial, or something else?

A Woman Prepared Jesus for Burial
Remind participants that one of the indictments of Jesus by the authorities had to do with whom he admitted to table fellowship. In this passage, he eats with Simon the leper and someone of the wrong gender, confirming the authorities' accusation.

Elicit from the group the contrasts related to money in this story and in Judas' betrayal, and record their responses on a large sheet of paper. Then remind participants of the passage cited in Chapter 6 of the study where Jesus insists Scripture trumps *corban* (devoting one's means to religious causes at the expense of providing for one's elders). Invite the group to compare this teaching with what happened when the woman demonstrated extravagant devotion and was criticized for wasting money that could have been devoted to the poor. What does the group make of the contrasts here? What might the study writer mean by the statement that "assisting the poor should not be an excuse not to do good for Jesus" (page 65)?

The Final Meal With the Disciples
Ask the group to name the two interrelated events mentioned by the study writer (Jesus' prediction of the treacherous act and the interpretation of the bread and wine).

What connections does the group see between the act of dipping bread in the bowl together and Jesus' mystical interpretation of the meaning of the bread and wine? What is the new covenant? Ask someone to read aloud Zechariah 13:7-9. How does the group respond to the idea that the one striking the shepherd is God?

Jesus' Prayer

Mark's account of the events in Gethsemane is another opportunity to observe the inattentiveness and cluelessness of the disciples. What explanation can the group find for such a response from the same disciples who witnessed the Transfiguration? Can group members remember times when in their own denial of a situation, they failed to provide the comfort and support another person needed?

Jesus' Trials and the Significance of the Crucifixion

Invite the group to act as "appeals judges" for the trials of Jesus. Form three small groups or pairs, and assign a trial to each. Ask participants to read the Bible passage and the related material in the study. As a total group, fill in the chart with the information about the trials. Then ask the group to discuss whether the results met the burden of proof for convicting Jesus. What, other than proper trial procedure, was at play in these trials?

Ask participants to name the aspects of the Crucifixion that point to the political nature of Jesus' death. How did the message of Jesus about God's intent for shalom for the world pose a threat to the *Pax Romana*?

The Meaning of Jesus' Death

Assign to each of the same three small groups or pairs one of the events of hope the study writer names, asking them to read the relevant verses in the Bible and the information in the study. Together, discuss the following: What does each event signify? What is the sign of hope? Why does the study writer say that "Jesus' death was the beginning of a revisioning of the status quo" (page 70? How do you respond to the idea that Jesus died not because he had to die, but because his death was a consequence of his prophetic vision?

Live the Story

Invite the group to look again at the questions they chose to include on the large sheet of paper. Which questions have been answered in the session? Which remain unresolved? The study states that Jesus' death and the way in which he lived his life are signs of hope to anyone who chooses "to do justice, love kindness, and walk humbly with . . . God" (Micah 6:8). Can hope and the idea that sacrifice is a part of the Christian life coexist?

Close by reading aloud Howard Thurman's two meanings of the Crucifixion. Then have the group read Psalm 22 in unison.

8. Jesus' Burial and Resurrection
Mark 15:42–16:8 (compare 16:9-20)

Faith Focus
Mark's story challenged the followers of Jesus to go out from the empty tomb and begin anew in mission with the Spirit of Jesus in their midst. Like those early disciples, we can embrace as trustworthy the message that we will see Jesus, just as he told us.

Before the Session
Print on a large sheet of paper "How would you have reacted if an angelic being was telling you that Jesus had been raised? Would you have delivered his message or run away as the women did?" Participants will need paper and pencils or pens. Check your denominational hymnal to see if the Apostle's Creed and the Nicene Creed are included, or make copies of the creeds for participants. Gather drawing paper and colored felt-tip markers or crayons.

Claim Your Story
Ask participants to read the questions on the large sheet of paper. Remind them that from our two millennia-later perspective, we have the benefit of hindsight; we know the rest of the story. Ask them to try to put themselves in the shoes of the women coming to the tomb to anoint Jesus' body and to respond in writing to the questions. If they think their response to the second question would be something other than the two alternatives, they can write that instead.

Enter the Bible Story
The Burial of Jesus
Ask participants to contrast Roman and Jewish customs regarding the handling of the bodies of crucified criminals. Why would Joseph of Arimathea, a member of the Sanhedrin that had condemned Jesus to death, request Jesus' body for burial? Was it a pious act or the result of feelings of ambivalence? Was Joseph, like the legal expert to whom Jesus said, "You aren't far from God's kingdom" (Mark 12:34), still not completely committed to the call of Jesus? In what ways do we demonstrate a similarly tepid commitment to the call of Jesus?

Invite the group to read or recite both the Nicene Creed and the Apostle's Creed. Why was it important to early Christians to affirm that Jesus was not only dead, but buried? How is it important to Christians today?

The Surprise Absence From the Tomb
Invite participants to choose any one of the other three Gospel accounts of the Resurrection (Matthew 28:1-10; Luke 24:1-12; John 20:1-18) and read it silently. Then ask them to name who each Gospel indicates was the first to get the news of Jesus' resurrection, and from whom. List these on a large sheet of paper for each Gospel. Then read Mark 16:1-8 and compare Mark's account with the others. Why did the early church try to

diminish the role of women in Jesus' mission, particularly their pivotal role as first witnesses to the Resurrection? What, in the group's opinion, is the status of women in the church today? Are there places where there are still attempts to muffle their voices and diminish their role?

The Promised Regathering and Ending—What's Missing

The study writer poses the theory that Mark's ending in 16:1-8 was enigmatic because he was writing to those who knew a part of the story already; Mark did not need to write a happy ending. How does the group respond to this explanation?

What key events does the study indicate Mark omitted that are included in the other Gospels? Why is it that each Gospel's ending has unique features? What is the significance of the translation "He has been raised" (Mark 16:6, CEB and NRSV) as opposed to "He has risen" (RSV, NIV)? Does it matter whether the Resurrection was by Jesus' own power or by God's initiative? Discuss.

The Longer Endings

Ask half the group to read the "shorter ending" and the section of the commentary in the study entitled "The Longer Endings of the Gospel of Mark (16:9; 16:9-2)" and the other half of the group to do the same for the "longer ending." What do participants think are the reasons these endings were added? If they could write their own ending, what might they include? Why? For what questions would they try to find answers?

Live the Story

The study writer suggests that Mark's message of hope was illustrated by the empty tomb rather than by a resurrection and that the promise of regathering is a call to community. We are challenged to leave the empty tomb and imagine where we will move forward in mission in community.

Distribute drawing paper and colored markers or crayons. Invite participants to head the paper "The Empty Tomb" or to create a simple line drawing of the tomb. Ask them to imagine what God may be calling your faith community to do and be in mission. What steps might you be called to take to further an aspect of mission already begun or to go forth in an entirely new direction? Ask participants either to create line drawings or to use phrases to express the response your faith community may be called to make. In what ways might newness be breaking in? Encourage participants to consider what part God may be calling them to play.